Demystifying Organisation Development

INTRAC NGO Management and Policy Series

1. *Institutional Development and NGOs in Africa: Policy Perspectives for European Development Agencies* Alan Fowler with Piers Campbell and Brian Pratt

2. *Governance, Democracy and Conditionality: What Role for NGOs?* Edited by Andrew Clayton

3. *Measuring the Process: Guidelines for Evaluating Social Development* David Marsden, Peter Oakley and Brian Pratt

4. *Strengthening the Capacity of NGOs: Cases of Small Enterprise Development Agencies in Africa* Caroline Sahley

5. *NGOs, Civil Society and the State: Building Democracy in Transitional Countries* Edited by Andrew Clayton

6. *Outcomes and Impact: Evaluating Change in Social Development* Peter Oakley, Brian Pratt and Andrew Clayton

7. *Demystifying Organisation Development: Practical Capacity Building Experiences of African NGOs* Rick James

8. *Direct Funding from a Southern Perspective: Strengthening Civil Society?* INTRAC

9. *NGO Responses to Urban Poverty: Service Providers or Partners in Planning?* Caroline Sahley and Brian Pratt

10. *Financial Management for Development: Accounting and Finance for the Non-specialist in Development Organisations* John Cammack

11. *NGOs Engaging with Business: A World of Difference and a Difference to the World* Simon Heap

12. *Power and Partnership? Experiences of NGO Capacity-Building* Edited by Rick James

13. *Evaluating Empowerment: Reviewing the Concept and Practice* Edited by Peter Oakley

14. *Knowledge, Power and Development Agendas: NGOs North and South* Emma Mawdsley, Janet Townsend, Gina Porter and Peter Oakley

15. *People and Change: Exploring Capacity-Building in NGOs* Rick James

16. *Changing Expectations?: The Concept and Practice of Civil Society in International Development* Edited by Brian Pratt

17. *The Development of Civil Society in Central Asia* Janice Giffen and Lucy Earle with Charles Buxton

18. *Creativity and Constraint: Grassroots Monitoring and Evaluation and the International Aid Arena* Edited by Lucy Earle

Demystifying Organisation Development

Practical Capacity-Building Experiences of African NGOs

Rick James

INTRAC NGO Management and Policy Series No. 7

An INTRAC Publication

INTRAC:

A Summary Description
INTRAC, the International NGO Training and Research Centre, was set up in 1991 to provide specially designed training, consultancy and research services to organisations involved in international development and relief. Our goal is to improve NGO performance by exploring policy issues and by strengthening management and organisational effectiveness.

First published in 1998 in the UK by
INTRAC
PO Box 563
Oxford
OX2 6RZ
United Kingdom

Tel: +44 (0)1865 201851
Fax: +44 (0)1865 201852
Email: info@intrac.org
Website: www.intrac.org

ISBN 10: 1-897748-35-3
ISBN 13: 978-1-897748-35-0

Designed and produced by
Jerry Burman
Tel: +44 (0)1803 409754

Printed in Great Britain by
Biddles Ltd., Kings Lynn, Norfolk

Acknowledgements

This publication would not have been possible without the support and efforts of a number of different people. First and foremost I would like to thank all the OD consultants; Lynette Maart, James Taylor, Carol-Ann Foulis, William Ogara, Daudi Waithaka, Mosi Kisare, David Harding, and Liz Goold, who made time in their busy schedules to reflect and write up case studies of an OD intervention.

The research involved the following up of these cases through visits to most of the NGOs concerned. Semi-structured interviews were conducted with staff at ABA, TUBA, TTO, Olive, Fellowship of Churches, CRC and Sende. The input from these people was invaluable to the process and greatly appreciated.

A number of Northern NGO staff: Chris Roche, Sarah Hughes, Sally Burrows, Ricardo Wilson-Grau, Han de Groot, Ellen Sprenger, Martine Benshop-Jansen, Peter de Keijzer, Stan van Wichelen, Rikke Norhlind, Calle Almedal, Bodil Ravn, Anders Tunold, Fernando Grantham, and Marion Keil all gave of their time to be interviewed too.

Funding for this research was very generously given by DANIDA and Norwegian Church Aid. Without their support none of this research would have been possible and so much recognition should go to them. Their commitment is an example of how some enlightened donors are putting resources into learning and reflection rather than just action. However, they are not responsible for any of the opinions expressed in this publication. Responsibility rests with INTRAC.

I have been substantially aided in this project by advisory support from a number of sources, but in particular from DIS (Norway) and CDRA (South Africa). Ivar Evensmo of DIS was very helpful in the planning of the work, the identification of literature, and gave ongoing comments on drafts throughout the process. James Taylor of CDRA helped particularly with the planning and structuring of the research as well as contributing two case studies. INTRAC Associates, John Hailey, David Harding and Alan Fowler all provided extremely useful ideas and comments at different stages of the work. Bill Cooke of IDPM Manchester helped considerably with the literature search.

The staff at INTRAC have been very supportive in many ways with ideas, challenges and administration. I would like to thank in particular Brian, Liz, Sara, Paul, Dani, Sue, and Martina for all their time amidst their busy schedules.

The illustrations come from Bill Crooks of Tear Fund who alerted us to the problem that many staff of Northern NGOs do not have time to read!

I would also like to thank Augustine, Angela, Joyce, Joseph, Wilson and Timothy – for proving to me in Malawi that OD consultants can be effective even after limited experience and formation.

To Cathy, for her constant support and love and inspiration.

Contents

Introduction

The significant global changes in the last decade are offering NGOs (non-government organisations) world-wide unparalleled opportunities to make a considerable contribution to the development of their countries. NGOs are being given more resources and greater responsibilities. The growing emphasis on the promotion of 'civil society institutions' as a countervailing power to the state in the democratisation process is expanding further the role and funding of NGOs.

As the roles and expectations of NGOs expand, so the need for capacity-building is increasingly identified so much so that 'capacity development has become a rallying cry – it is being heralded as the missing link in development' (Bussuyt 1995:1). Within the field of NGO capacity-building, Organisation Development (OD) consultancy is being seen as a key approach. OD is being prioritised as a key development strategy by a number of major European NGOs such as Novib, Hivos, Bilance, Oxfam, Norwegian Church Aid, and Danchurchaid. A recent survey of Northern[1] NGO approaches to capacity-building of Southern[2] NGOs revealed that 'Organisation Development and Renewal' is currently the main capacity-building priority for Northern NGOs (James 1998).

THE ADVANTAGES OF OD CONSULTANCY

The Potential Benefits of OD Consultancy
OD consultancy is a potentially effective approach to NGO capacity-building for a number of reasons.

OD focuses on organisations. In the past Northern NGOs have tended to view Southern NGOs as little more than discrete technical projects. The recent realisation of the importance of dealing with organisational issues has come from a

---

[1] Throughout this publication, Northern NGOs will be used to refer to NGOs from the OECD countries (recognising that this division is far from geographically accurate)

[2] Southern NGOs correspond to NGOs from traditional aid recipient countries.

dual recognition that strong local organisations are critical for the development of a healthy civil society whilst at the same time appreciating that 'in developing countries there is considerable lack of organisational and management capacities and the lack of effective organisation is a serious bottleneck to development' (Kiggundu in Kaijage 1993:4).

OD recognises the complexity of organisations. The experience of NGO capacity-building to date shows it to be a difficult, dynamic and long-term process. This is not surprising given that 'if one truly wishes to understand an organisation, it is much wiser to start from the assumption that they are complex, ambiguous and paradoxical' (Morgan 1986:322).

OD stresses the importance of being able to adapt to the changing environment. The NGO environment is increasingly being described as 'turbulent' with major changes in funding and NGO roles forcing NGOs to adapt quickly.

OD emphasises the importance of dealing with 'core' organisational issues. Many NGOs and donors recognise that many of the organisational needs of NGOs lie deeper than just a lack of resources and skills as, 'NGOs are struggling with questions of leadership, motivation, direction, strategy, monitoring and evaluation, structure, systems, procedures, conflict and teamwork' (CDRA 1992/3:9). These questions are increasingly recognised as being critical for organisational strengthening.

The Limitations of Other Approaches to Capacity-Building
The most popular and traditional approach to strengthening NGO capacity is undoubtedly training. Many of the European NGOs interviewed in the course of this research expressed frustration with the lack of impact of the previous training-based approaches to capacity-building and agreed with Fowler and Waithaka that 'some 10 years of a training dominated approach to capacity-building have shown its severe limitations in improving organisational effectiveness' (Fowler and Waithaka 1995:3). While training can be effective for bringing in new ideas, it is less effective at helping people let go of old ways of doing things – a vital part of an organisational change. Furthermore, individuals are usually trained outside the organisation in an artificial context and then often face the problem of re-entry into an untrained organisation sometimes leading to frustration, paralysis and demotivation. While training is a tangible and seductive package, it often allows organisations the opportunity to avoid taking responsibility for addressing the deeper issues.

Some of these issues can be illustrated using the simple INTRAC onion skin model for understanding NGO capacity.

The outside layer of the 'onion skin' represents the physical and financial resources which an NGO needs – money, buildings, vehicles, equipment. Inside that layer are the human skills required to carry out the activities – the individual staff competencies and abilities. Inside that the structures and systems (such as monitoring and evaluation systems, personnel systems, financial management systems) needed to make an organisation work. Inside that the vision, purpose and strategy of the NGO – what it wants to achieve and how. Right at the heart of an organisation lies the core of an NGO: its identity, values, beliefs, culture, motivation and theory of development.

THE ONION SKIN APPROACH!

This model shows the inter-relationship between the different elements of an organisation's capacity and how training is often limited to changes at the level of skills and competencies.

It is clear that a more in-depth process of fostering organisational change is necessary. It is also clear that this must be done in a way in which ownership for the change process must be firmly in the hands of the organisation concerned. Traditionally, development consultancy has favoured an 'expert' approach in which the consultant diagnoses the problems and develops the solutions for the organisation. For example, ESAMI (East and Southern African Management Institute), admit that:

> in the past ESAMI has used conventional (consultant engineering models) to diagnose and design systems and structures, but ... experience has revealed the conventional approaches ... fail miserably, are poorly implemented, are discontinued and impose unacceptably large burdens on organisations resources ... They rarely produce lasting impact (Mbise and Shirma in Kaijage 1993:143)

OD consultancy, which offers a much more process-oriented approach of facilitating the organisation to diagnose its own problems and develop its own solutions, appears to present a viable alternative to traditional and largely unsuccessful attempts at organisational change.

OD consultancy has the advantage of being immediately attractive to NGOs as its underlying values of participation, empowerment and working together are consistent with NGO values and beliefs. Many European NGOs interviewed felt that OD was in fashion because it is a natural consequence of the outworking of NGO policies and philosophy. One agency described OD as a *'logical step having been supporting organisations rather than just projects over the last 10–15 years'* while another stated that *'OD is a condition sine qua non for sustainable development'* because *'to implement development activities in a sustainable way you need strong organisations'*.

There is also the expectation from some quarters that, not only will stronger partners enable Northern NGOs to fulfil their mission more effectively, but that stronger partners will reduce the workload on Northern NGO staff – many of whom feel overstretched by large portfolios of 'difficult and time-consuming' partners.

'WILL ODC REDUCE PROJECT OFFICER WORKLOAD?'

THE AIM OF THIS PUBLICATION

While this ODC approach is increasingly popular with NGOs, there had been almost no analysis of the practice and effectiveness of it, nor on the critical variables and constraints that determine its success. Much of Northern NGO policy and practice is being made in a vacuum of ignorance. This publication aims to contribute to filling that vacuum.

INTRAC undertook an 18-month research project in Eastern and Southern Africa to provide **Northern NGO policy-makers and programme officers** with a greater understanding of:

- What is OD Consultancy?
- What can ODC achieve?
- What cannot be achieved by ODC?
- What prevents or helps it to achieve its desired impact?
- Where does it work well and where it does not work well?
- How can NGOs use ODC or support it?
- How do we develop the supply of OD consultants?
- How do we measure the impact?
- How do we manage the process?

The aim is that Northern NGOs will be able to take more considered and effective decisions regarding how to strengthen their partners.

This publication is based on the findings of that research project (see Appendix 1 for methodology). The research examined nine case studies of OD consultancy as practised with NGOs, complementing visits to the NGOs concerned with semi-structured interviews with Northern NGO staff and African OD consultants. The scope of the research and the nature of the subject did impose a number of limitations on the research which should be borne in mind. For example, it was not possible to compare the effectiveness of OD consultancy with other capacity-building approaches especially given the serious definitional difficulties with OD (as we shall see in the next chapter); the sample of OD cases was limited both in number and geographic scope; it proved extremely difficult to overcome the inherent problems of attribution and contextual influences to evaluate 'objectively' the impact of an OD intervention. Finally the scope of the research did not permit questioning of the assumption that 'strengthened capacity of NGOs will have a positive impact on social change and development'. Issues of resources and access prevented significant evaluation of the OD consultancies at the level of ultimate beneficiary.

The Structure of the Publication

This publication is divided into four parts. Part 1 looks at some of the theoretical, conceptual and historical background to OD in order to understand better this overworked term. Part 2 grounds this theory by providing the reader with descriptions of practical experiences of OD consultancies with NGOs in Africa. Part 3 analyses these experiences in order to understand better the OD process in reality and to ascertain whether OD consultancy actually builds NGO capacity. The main factors which influence the success or otherwise of an OD intervention are identified along with key issues in OD which remain. Part 4 concludes by applying these lessons and implications to the day-to-day work of Northern NGOs.

Note on Style:
Unreferenced quotations in italics are taken from personal interviews during the research.

Practical men in authority who believe themselves to be quite exempt from any intellectual influences, are usually the slaves of some defunct economist (Keynes quoted in Edwards 1996b:30)

Part One

The Theory of OD

Chapter 1

The Nature of OD

INTRODUCTION

One of the major approaches to planned organisation change in the last 30 years has been, what is loosely termed, Organisation Development (OD). Originating in the USA in the 1960s, OD soon became a very diverse but ill-defined field. There is no single OD philosophy, nor one OD textbook to consult. The Addison-Wesley OD Series of more than 30 publications over the last 20 years indicates that 'diversity and innovation remain at the heart of the series' (Addison-Wesley OD Series:xvii). By 1974 one survey by the Institute of Personnel Management quoted no less than 50 separate definitions. The 'elastic' nature of OD can even be seen in specific OD interventions which may themselves change considerably over time. The lack of tight boundaries has the benefit of allowing diversity of opinion in a complex field and has also enabled OD to evolve significantly in order to meet the changing needs of organisations as well as address some of its own internal weaknesses.

The term OD has recently burst onto the NGO landscape as a by-product of the general recognition of the need for stronger non-government organisations to foster effective relief and development. It has become the fashionable concept of the late 1990s amongst NGOs, but is being used by many NGOs with careless abandon to mean whatever they want it to mean. It is very important to appreciate the different influences which have shaped OD as a diverse discipline.

THE DEVELOPMENT OF OD

What are the Roots of OD?
Early management theory was built on the work of Frederick Taylor during the 1920s and 1930s. Coming from an engineering background, Taylor's theory of management was a rational, technical framework where organisations and peo-

ple could and should be controlled like machines. This approach is sometimes called 'scientific' management.

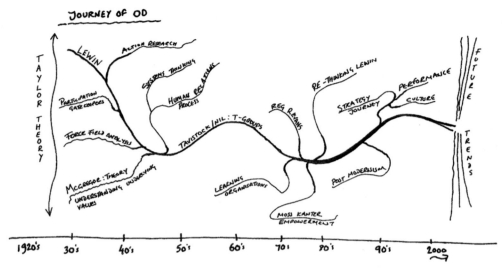

The OD Journey of Life

In contrast to this mechanistic approach to organisations, a group of behavioural scientists in the United States during the 1940s and 1950s began developing their own systems for facilitating management development and organisational effectiveness based on a shared commitment to democratic values within organisations. They focused on 'here and now' group dynamics exercises (such as T-groups) and in 1946 founded the National Training Laboratories Institute of Applied Behavioural Science. One of the main influences on this process was Karl Lewin whose work on the dynamics of the change process earned him the title of 'the intellectual father of contemporary theories of applied behavioural science' (Cooke 1996 a:6). One of the core principles to emerge from his work is that 'we are likely to modify our own behaviour when we **participate in problem analysis and solution identification** and are likely to carry out decisions we have helped to make'. His classic contributions of a three phase approach to change (unfreezing, moving, refreezing) and force-field analysis (working with the flow rather than against it) have had a profound influence on OD practice.

This influence was complemented by John Collier's development of **action research** in which it was discovered that a fundamental principle of action is that it is informed by research with its sequential steps of data collection / feedback / data analysis / action steps. This work was applied by people such as Likert who began to summarise and report back data collected from questionnaires that assessed employee attitudes and morale.

Another stream which led into the development of OD came from McGregor's work on Theory X and Theory Y in which he outlined how much of scientific management principles were based on negative assumptions of peoples' behaviour. He advocated a focus instead on their **potentials through team-working and joint problem-solving.**

Meanwhile in the UK, the Tavistock Institute was developing its work on socio-technical systems and **open-systems theories** of organisation. The work on open systems emphasised the importance of looking at the 'whole' picture of organisations and seeing them as a complex series of interconnected sub-systems.

Since its earliest days, OD has been evolving, and no more so than in the last 20 years. Some of the recent influences on OD include the neo-liberalism of the late 1980s and the increasingly competitive organisational environment. As an adaptation to this changed context, OD has recognised the importance of dealing with issues of **task, strategy and performance.** OD has had to become more responsive to the strategic needs of the organisation and its interrelationship with the environment as 'interpersonal issues are seen as relevant by most client systems only in so far as they influence task accomplishment' (Schein 1987:51). OD is therefore no longer concerned only with 'micro-interventions' such as team-building (though these are still very important), but also with macro issues of strategic planning, reward systems, management structures and information systems. OD is now integrating structure versus processes issues; performance versus people issues.

OD has broadened its approach. In the past OD had been

unconsciously assuming the only thing of interest is the people ... OD tried to ignore technology and the business realities of the organisation and the environment, ... but OD has become more comfortable with the fact that the whole system must be the object of the change. (Vaill quoted in Lippitt et al. 1985:144)

OD has also shifted from dealing primarily with an organisation's current problems towards helping organisations **envisage their future,** as encapsulated by Weisbord's work on Future Search Conferences (Weisbord 1992).

Yet, on the other hand, while strategy is being given greater emphasis, **culture maintains its importance** in OD practice.

What has become clear to people involved in a fairly significant change in organisation strategy, or even more complicated its mission, is the fact that an organisation's culture usually has to be changed for the new strategy to work effectively. It is difficult if not impossible to implement a new strategy if the way of implementing the decisions remains the same. (Burke 1987:163)

There is recognition of the need to look deeper and discover why organisations are unable to strategise effectively and why morale is low. This still often involves cultural issues. How and whether organisations' cultures can be changed is the subject of much debate. While it is recognised that top-down impositions of new cultural practices have been largely ineffective, it is still thought that top leadership plays a pivotal role in the development of an organisation's culture.

Over the past 15 years there has been greater emphasis within OD on the **role of top management and leadership** in effecting organisational change. Previously the leadership has tended to be seen as having a strong negative power to obstruct OD intervention (a necessary evil), but increasingly they are being seen as the critical actors in the process. It is understood that OD must aim higher and develop effective rapport with top management and support the leadership role. Once again this shift reflects trends in wider society though some question whether this top-team focus is appropriate for the development world.

One of the most powerful recent influences on OD has come from writers like Vaill, Weisbord and Stacey who have emphasised the **turbulent nature of the environment** in which organisations are operating. The powerful influence of the external environment on the internal functioning of organisations is increasingly recognised. In a context when things are changing rapidly, the notion that 'refreezing' is desirable or even possible becomes an anachronism. They argue that there is a need to become more 'adaptive' to the constant change around them. This has been reinforced by other writers like Senge, Argyris and Schon who show how adaptive organisations must be learning continuously from their experience. Helping organisations become **'learning' organisations** has become a key aspect of OD writings and practice.

In the early days of OD (and still in some quarters today) the metaphor of OD as a journey was often used with an emphasis on destination. The stress on goals, direction, phases and steps implicitly implied that the change process is a rational, structured and linear journey. This was influenced to a great degree by the recognition that an organisation is unlikely to contract a consultant who suggests that the outcomes of change are uncertain and must be to a large extent discovered en route.

More recently wider cultural developments such as the rise of the 'new sciences' (principally chaos theory and quantum physics) have shifted the OD metaphor more towards **OD being an explorative, process-oriented journey,** where clear outcomes are not known in advance. While 'early OD emphasised destination, current practice seems to be more concerned with good seamanship and keeping the craft buoyant and picking a course between the many hazards' (McLean et al. 1982:125).

One useful summary of recent trends is given by Esper (1990:302–3):

From	To
Stable environments Lewin's models made sense	Constant unpredictable change Refreezing impossible/inappropriate
Problems solved with clear answers	Multiple stakeholders and conflicting needs Paradoxes to be coped with e.g. collaboration and competition
Micro perspective on individual	Macro perspective with focus on system
Solely process skills Goal: human values Location: periphery	Process skills to complement content expertise Goal: organisational effectiveness and fit with environment Location: OD mainstream
OD an end in itself – technique driven	OD means to an end of greater organisational effectiveness
OD problem-solving interventions Developmental change	OD the creation of preferred futures. Transformational change

OD has certainly not been a cloistered discipline that has remained aloof from shifts in broad applied social science thinking, political changes and management and organisation theory. OD has responded to a variety of sometimes cross-cutting influences. Its evolution has been both contested and differentiated with the pendulum swinging between the desire for 'harder', more control, task-oriented approaches to management while at the same time recognising that organisations and their environments are inherently more complex and dynamic than that and the consequent need to look beyond the formal to more informal and 'softer' elements.

What are the Underlying Values of OD?

Despite these shifts in OD, its philosophical underpinnings of helping the client system to help itself has remained constant. As with PRA (Participatory Rural Appraisal), its foundations are based on values of participation and process and, therefore, it is the attitude and behaviour of practitioners that make techniques effective, not the techniques themselves. To understand OD better and identify the agenda which it brings, it is important to investigate its underlying values and assumptions. Commonly cited values of OD are that:

- it is valuable to give opportunities to people to develop towards their full potential;
- people are human beings with complex sets of needs not just resources to be used;
- it emphasises values of openness, trust and collaborative effort;
- it seeks simultaneously to meet the needs of individuals and several systems/groups;
- it is grounded in immediate experience 'here and now' data;
- it emphasises feelings and emotions as well as ideas and concepts;
- individual participants are involved as subject and object in action research;
- it puts reliance on group controls for choice and change;
- it emphasises interaction.

(Golembiewski quoted in Srinivas 1995)

DEFINITIONS OF OD

How well do Northern NGOs Understand OD?

Given the diverse and contested history of OD it is not surprising that European NGOs' understanding of OD (interviewed during the research project) was varied. While some of the respondents were far from clear what the subject was about, others displayed a well-developed understanding of OD. There was a recognition of some of the key elements in OD such as its process rather than expert consultancy nature; its view of organisations as integrated, whole entities; the importance of gender; and the goal of OD being to *'facilitate a process to develop the capacity of an NGO to manage its own change process'*.

Most agencies thought that the organisational understanding of OD had increased greatly in the last few years, with field offices often leading the way. Overall, however, there was still not a coherent organisational understanding of OD amongst any of the NGOs. Understanding was still very individually based with the most frequent response to questions about the meaning of OD being *'it depends on whom you ask'*.

Few agencies were either really clear what they meant by OD or had developed policies and strategies for OD (NCA being a notable exception). Even one of the most experienced agencies admitted, *'we have not defined it yet as an organisation and we use the term very loosely'*.

Despite the obvious drawbacks in not really knowing what you are doing, there appear to be a number of reasons why NGOs might want to keep the term OD vague and undefined.

- To access government funding. Some official donors such as NORAD for example explicitly support organisation development activities and so it is in Norwegian NGOs' interest to make such a definition as broad as possible.

- Coming to a coherent organisational understanding about a complex subject takes much time and effort, and unless it is a definite priority, it will be avoided.

- Keeping the definition of OD unclear enables NGOs to benefit from the internal and external recognition that they are involved in a fashionable area of development, while evading significant conflict with more established and traditional ways of working, such as project-based funding.

As a result, only a few European NGOs are making any attempt to understand, define or even practice OD. While there may be a diversity of definitions of OD (see Box 1.1), it is possible to highlight elements which are common to most OD definitions.

What are Common Definitions of OD?

Box 1.1 Common Definitions of OD

'OD is a response to change, a complex educational strategy intended to change the beliefs, attitudes, values and structure of organisations so that they can better adapt to new technologies, markets and challenges and to the dizzying rate of change itself' (Bennis 1966, quoted in McLean et al. 1982:84).

'an effort, planned, organisation-wide and managed from the top, to increase organisational effectiveness and health through planned interventions in the organisational processes using behavioural science knowledge' (Beckhard and Harris 1987).

'the applied behavioural science discipline that seeks to improve organisations through planned systematic, long-range efforts focused on the organisation culture and its human and social processes' (French and Bell 1984).

'OD is a process of people managing the culture of an organisation, rather than being managed by it' (French and Bell 1984:20).

'OD is a planned process of change in an organisations culture through the utilisation of behavioural science technologies, research and theory' (Burke 1987:11).

'OD is a system-wide application of behavioural science knowledge to the planned development and reinforcement of organisation strategies, structures and processes for achieving organisational effectiveness' (Huse and Cummings 1985:1).

'OD is the discipline of creating and applying processes aimed at developing the capacity of organisations, where capacity is seen as their increase in organisational awareness and consciousness such that the organisation is better able to take control of its own functions and future in a responsible manner' (CDRA 1995:26).

'The discipline by which people endeavour to bring organisational health by creating and applying processes which bring about the right balance of organisational structure, systems and ways of working, so as to enable the organisation to achieve its aims' (Mario van Boeschoten 1996, in OD Debate, Vol. 3 No.1 p. 3).

'the facilitation of an organisation's capacity to self-reflect, self-regulate and take control of its own processes of improvement and learning' (Kaplan 1996: 89).

'creating the conditions in which change can take place from within an organisation' (Hailey, 1994, INTRAC Training Materials).

What does INTRAC Understand by OD?

Towards an INTRAC Definition – Ten Core Ingredients of OD

The diversity of approaches to and definitions of OD reflects the diversity of understanding of organisations. INTRAC believes that there are some core elements in OD which form the basis of the framework for this publication. INTRAC believes in OD as a participatory and process-oriented approach which is in line with general participative approaches to development itself and also reflects the methods used by the case studies in this publication. It should be recognised that this stance may not necessarily be shared by all management writers or practitioners.

The following common elements of OD represent a set of ideals. In reality every situation is imperfect and one of compromise. In order to be able to work effectively, however, one must understand the OD ideal and negotiate and compromise from those principles. The aspirations of OD have shifted from the ambitious to the more modest and acquired greater realism. For example, while OD consultants may prefer to work with whole organisations, they also appreciate the value of intervening at a team or departmental level.

1. The goal of OD is not just that an organisation can solve its current problem today, but that it can be strengthened to solve its future problems too

OD stresses developing client capabilities for future problem solving. Most change efforts focus on solving existing problems in an organisation. Although this is one goal of OD, what distinguishes OD from other change efforts is its emphasis on developing clients' capabilities for problem solving after the consultant has gone. According to Schein, 'it is a critical assumption ... that problems will stay solved longer and be solved more effectively if the organisation solves those problems itself' (1988:7).

2. OD helps organisations become more able to 'learn'

Integrally related to being able to solve its future problems is the position that a key product of an OD intervention is that an NGO becomes more of a 'learning organisation'. It is argued that, in the present climate, change is so rapid that all you can do is develop capacity within an organisation to adapt to change: 'learning how to learn continuously and consciously from lived experience is the key if we are to avoid being overtaken and overwhelmed by environmental change' (Revens quoted in Blunt and Jones 1992:213). Becoming a 'learning organisation' is at the heart of OD and is one of the crucial tests of the effectiveness of an OD intervention. As Alan Fowler expresses it, 'if an OD process goes well, it never stops, but becomes a way of life' (1997:192).

3. OD sees organisations as whole systems of interrelated components, working with groups not just individuals

OD views organisations from a systems perspectives where issues, events and forces within organisations are not isolated but interrelated. Organisations are viewed holistically whereby a change in any one part of an organisation has an impact on the rest of the organisation. As Campbell says:

> All four (structure, staff, strategy, teams) have to be brought together in one strategy designed to improve the effectiveness of the organisation. This is what OD is all about: helping the NGO look at all aspects of the organisation in a coherent and comprehensive way. (1994:vi)

Furthermore OD is a process of people learning to change together not apart. The focus is on the development of groups and organisations. Individual development is promoted only when it is required to improve group functioning.

4. OD focuses on organisational culture

In recent years the importance of an organisation's 'culture' in determining how it functions has been increasingly emphasised. Culture can be defined as a 'pattern of learned underlying assumptions about how to behave' or in more colloquial language 'the way we do things round here'. Organisations are much more complex than the formal aspects which can be easily seen 'above the water-line' such as the organisational charts, the job descriptions, the mission statements or strategic plans. The ways in which organisations perform are often more influenced by the informal things which occur 'below the water-line' such as the way people relate unofficially, the political manoeuvring, the personalities involved, the ways decisions are made.

The analogy of a hippo or an iceberg is often used to illustrate this reality. In more literary terms, Schein likens culture to lily pads:

> There you can see the lilies floating on top of the pond ... but you do not see the roots that may go down 10–15 feet, deeply bedded down in the mud that made the lily pad grow. If you do not get down into these roots and down into the mud, you do not understand the whole process'. (Schein quoted in Info-line 1988:5)

OD stresses the centrality of culture to organisational change. Burke (1987) states that one of the three criteria for deciding whether an intervention can be classified as OD is whether it brings about a change in organisational culture. This is on the premise that 'the overarching determinant of how organisations work is the culture that is evolved in the organisation' (Schein quoted in Blunt

1995:213). The poor performance of most top-down corporate culture change programmes, however, has led to recent emphasis that 'rather than trying to manage culture though culture change programs, you should consider your cultural context whenever you contemplate or carry out organisational change' (Hatch 1997:235).

It is also increasingly recognised in OD that politics and vested interests form a very considerable part of the informal organisation. The OD gospel of openness, trust and authenticity is losing some of its political *naïveté* and developing greater awareness of the sources of power within organisation and how they must be recognised and used to bring about change.

5. OD is about conscious, not accidental change

Organisations develop, change and grow irrespective of any intervention. There are inherent life processes which occur naturally. OD, or perhaps more accurately OD interventions, are conscious attempts to help organisations become more effective in their work and adaptive to their environment. This conscious approach to change shows that 'while change is inevitable, change that happens to an organisation can be distinguished from change that is planned by organisational members' (Huse and Cummings 1985:19). In the past OD has been defined as a process of planned change in which the nature of the change is defined and owned by the organisation. Controls and levers, such as indicators and planning tools, are increasingly popular in encouraging organisational change but it has been questioned whether change can really be controlled and planned – the idea of OD as a conscious attempt to foster change is seen as more realistic.

6. OD encompasses a process of collaborative diagnosis based on action research

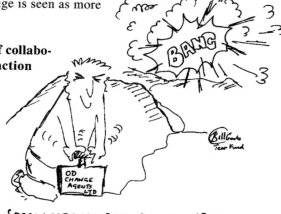

It is difficult to overstate the importance of diagnosis in the change process in determining the priority issues; the type of intervention needed; whether there is sufficient internal commitment to change. As Albrecht says, 'prescription without diagnosis is malpractice whether in

'ORGANISATIONAL DEVELOPMENT IS ABOUT PLANNED NOT ACCIDENTAL CHANGE'

medicine or management' (quoted in Info-Line 1988:7). This diagnosis should be a process of self-appraisal by the client (often facilitated), not expert, external appraisal where the consultant does the diagnosis.

OD is based on an action research model of continual data collection, analysis and feedback for collective awareness – on the assumption that for effective change to occur, issues and solutions should be owned internally not displaced. This is underpinned by a normative, re-educative change strategy 'which works with the heart and the head by supporting learning processes that accept the psychological resistance to the change of fundamental attitudes' (Rao and Kellerher 1995:3).

'SELF-DIAGNOSIS'

7. OD focuses on people, not physical resources

The emphasis of OD is on human resources, their motivation, utilisation and integration within the organisation and is therefore NOT about purchasing new equipment, raising money or redesigning the project. Organisations are seen to be made up of a collection of human beings interacting together. Change in peoples' behaviour is a major concern and therefore collaboration is stressed not only as a useful process, but also as a key outcome.

8. OD uses both micro- and increasingly macro-activities

OD uses a variety of planned programmatic activities designed to help an organisation become more effective. Recently there has been an increasing shift from process-related micro interventions such as group dynamics, work design, leadership, to more performance-related macro-activities focusing on strategy, structure and relations to environment reflecting senior executive interest in task issues rather than relationship issues.

There is widening recognition of the need to take into account the external environment in diagnosing the health of an organisation, especially as the NGO environment is being seen as increasingly chaotic.

9. OD has an ongoing process nature

Because we live in a state of continuous change and because addressing issues of culture may involve long-standing deeply engrained patterns of behaviour, OD is not a one-shot solution. It is a long-term, systemic process striving towards greater effectiveness through a series of interventions over time. Some distinguish authentic OD on the length of interventions and say that a little OD may even be a dangerous thing as 'small amounts of OD training may serve to surface problems, but do not allow for sufficient time to let the staff deal constructively and thoroughly with problems' (Fullan et al. quoted in Walters 1990:215).

10. OD focuses on improving the organisational effectiveness as defined by the organisation itself

OD must meet a felt need of the organisation and have an end of improved performance, not be an end in itself.

What is the Difference between Organisation Development, Institutional Development and Capacity-Building?

We have shown that our definition of OD involves ten core ingredients, but there is no set OD recipe. The proportions of each ingredient is likely to vary between different OD interventions. It is worth noting at this point that our definition of OD is distinct from the inherent and natural process of development which all organisations (and people) go through to some degree, from birth often with a charismatic pioneer (sometimes called dependence); to a phase of delegation and differentiation (sometimes called independence); to a phase of integration (sometimes known as interdependence). This development occurs without necessarily any outside input. OD interventions in this process take place and are often useful in helping organisations deal with the tensions and crises as organisations get 'stuck' towards the end of one stage and involves helping them move to the next one (though they are also important in helping organisations manage their current stage of development).

In the NGO world as well as the academic literature, OD is often used to describe an intervention which might be more accurately called OD consultancy (ODC) as consultancy is the prime intervention used. People tend to use these words synonymously which sometimes creates some confusion. In this publication we shall try and use ODC (or OD interventions or OD processes) as much as possible though recognising the tendency to follow conventional practice.

There are other 'organisational' interventions which in and of themselves would not fit our description of OD. Some of these might fall under the term technical inputs such as technical skills training or advice on establishing computer/finance systems; others under management assistance such as management skills training courses. We believe these are important capacity-building interventions which might be **part of an OD process** (if they were identified by the organisation through their own assessment as being critical), but if used in isolation they would not constitute our definition of OD.

Capacity-building is therefore broader than OD and as well as technical and management inputs might include interventions such as relationship development through networking, mediation and exchanges. Appropriate funding is even seen by some as capacity-building.

Another much used phrase which needs some definition and differentiation from OD is Institutional Development (ID). The difference then between ID and OD is derived from the differences between institutions and organisations. According to Fowler, institutions are 'stable patterns of behaviour that are recognised and valued by society' (1992:14–15). These may be organisations such as the central bank or diffuse like the institution of money or marriage. Organisations are seen to be purposeful, structured, role-bound social units.

ID therefore is concerned with the wider changes in societies and seeks to initiate changes outside the boundaries of a single organisation. It is about effecting macro-changes in the structure of society and economic relations and creating the enabling environment in civil society for development to take place.

OD is restricted more to changes within an organisation even if those changes then have a wider impact on ID.

In practice OD and ID are extremely interconnected as OD with NGOs is one of the main strategies for achieving ID. Rondinelli (1989) goes even further by saying that OD is a precondition for ID. According to EASUN, 'OD is considered more as a means for institutional development and the broader aims of the NGO sector in society' (EASUN 1996c:5) and 'a complete and meaningful OD intervention for an NGO, therefore, will remain tuned to its social sustainabilty, including issues of legitimacy, methodologies applied in programme implementation, the mechanisms of accountability to its local constituency and the vision of itself in relations with its institutional environment' (ibid.:9).

Chapter 2

OD Consultancy

There is nothing more difficult to execute, nor more dubious of success, nor more dangerous to administer than to introduce a new order of things, for he who introduces it has all those who profit from the old order as his enemies, and he has only lukewarm allies in all those who might profit from the new. (Machiavelli, 1513, *The Prince*)

INTRODUCTION

In the previous chapter we traced the differentiated history of OD as a discipline, identified some of its underlying values and concluded with INTRAC's working definition of OD encapsulating ten core elements. In this chapter we will examine the process of implementing OD interventions, largely through OD consultancy. We will initially look at the consultancy spectrum, noting how our definition of OD tends to sit more comfortably towards the process end of the scale; we will find out what processes OD consultancies tend to follow; identify common OD methods and tools; examine the different roles available to OD consultants and then analyse the characteristics and qualities needed by effective OD consultants.

OD CONSULTANCY

What is OD Consultancy?

The prime methodology for implementing OD is consultancy. Consultancy can be defined as 'what should happen when someone with a problem or difficulty seeks help to solve that problem or resolve that difficulty from someone who has special skill' (Cockman et al. 1992:2).

Consultants are hired to facilitate change in organisations. They are there to influence and advise people, to help them and persuade them to do things differently. Consultancy is an appropriate approach when there is a genuine need for specific skills to be made available in specific situations for limited periods of time. Consultancy benefits from the flexibility of consultants being able to respond more quickly to provide new services tailored to individual needs. Consultants can bring specialisation, mobility, a variety of services and direct accountability for quality, yet they operate without any formal authority over anyone.

OD consultancy is a particular form of consultancy which can be differentiated from more traditional consultancy interventions in using the Expert Process spectrum.

Our definition of ODC is different from prescriptive and problem-solving management consultancy – sometimes known as the 'mafia model'. Task-focused consultancies can be effective in tackling particular organisational or operational issues, but are unlikely to initiate organisation-wide changes. For example, using a consultant to advise on a computer system is an organisational systems consultancy, but is unlikely to meet many of the criteria outlined above. It is common to see ODC as nearer the 'process' or 'client-centred' end of the consultancy spectrum, not the 'expert' end.

OD tends to be differentiated from other forms of organisational consultancy in the way it is done, rather than necessarily the content alone. For example, a strategic planning exercise may be done in an outside prescriptive way leaving the organisation as incapacitated as before, and therefore share little in common with principles of OD, whereas another strategic planning exercise may be facilitated in such a way as to be entirely consistent with these principles.

As Allan Kaplan says there is a paradox, 'OD consultants are expected to bring expertise ... yet valued equally for their opposite ability to withhold this expertise in facilitating the organisation through its own process of developing its own ability to solve its own problems' (1996:76).

While the process/expert spectrum is a useful distinction, current thinking claims that the role of OD consultants is expanding to include the expert role and is seen as 'falling along the entire continuum from client centred to consultant centred' (Huse and Cummings 1985:403).

The Expert Process Consultancy Continuum

Consultancy Method	Expert	Process
Aim	One-off problem solving	Ongoing ability of organisation to solve its own problems
Assumptions	Problem easily diagnosed Problem not too hot to handle	Problem not well understood
Nature of problem	Technical Nuts and bolts	Cultural Learning/ adaptation
Scope of Problem	Single part of organisation	Whole organisation
Nature of diagnosis	By client	By client through consultant's facilitation
Expertise required	System-specific	Process facilitation
Remedy from	Consultant	By client through consultant's facilitation
Change Strategy	Coercion?	Consultation
Diagnosis/ Intervention	Separate	As one
Length of time needed	Short	Long
Length of time available	Short	Long
Nature of input	One time	Periodic
Focus	Formal organisation	Informal organisation
Intervention outputs	Reports and recommendations	Creating new ways of working
Risks	Lack of ownership and inaction. Solution not understood	Neglect of task

How do you Know if ODC is Needed?

Burke outlined a number of symptoms to ascertain whether ODC is needed (in Hanson and Lubin 1995:53):

- the same problems keep recurring;
- many efforts have been tried to solve the problem, but none work;
- morale and job satisfaction are low;
- high staff turnover or absenteeism;
- closed communication and a sense of isolation;
- apathy and resistance to change and innovation;
- avoidance of conflict;
- decision-making not shared;
- little ownership of organisational problems;
- rapid changes in the external environment.

Info-line (1988) also produced a checklist for determining if OD is needed.

- Is the organisation undergoing transition from one stage of growth to another?

- Does the organisation lack direction?

- Is there a sense of unrealised potential?

- Is the organisation undergoing some form of identity crisis?

- Is the organisation clinging to obsolete services, practices or products?

- Is the organisation experiencing low morale/staff turnover?

- Has the organisation grown very quickly?

- Are there conflicts about future direction?

- Has the organisation experienced major changes in its environment/technology?

- Is the organisation bogged down with inflexible rules, regulations and directives?

- Are there people in place hindering progress?

The more yes answers, the more likely the need for organisational change.

THE OD CONSULTING PROCESS

What is the Process of ODC?
While there are many different models of the process of OD consultancy, there tend to be broad similarities of approach. David Scott of ODISA outlines one such model:

(adapted from 'Managing the Process of Change', David Scott, CDRA 1996)

<u>Orientation</u>
1. First Contact and Building a Relationship
In response to a letter or phone call an appointment is usually made by the consultant to meet the client or group of people concerned. Just as with any meeting, judgements are made on first sight and it is important not to overlook the social phase of building a relationship and establishing trust. It is also necessary at this stage for the consultant to clarify the nature of the problem, trying to get down to the client's real question which might not be the presenting one. The temptation is to gloss over this initial, critical stage, which should culminate in contracting and 'probably all consultants would agree that problems arising in later stages of an assignment can be traced back to poor initial contracting or failure to renegotiate the contract as circumstances change' (Phillips and Shaw 1984:52).The purpose of contracting is therefore to make explicit the expectations of both parties so that neither side is disappointed as well as to ensure ownership of the process.

2. Data Collection
There is often a need to build a bigger picture by collecting more data and speaking to the people who are directly concerned. As well as becoming familiar with the formal aspects of the organisation, the consultant needs to get a feel for the more informal aspects such as issues of power, values, identity and culture. This information should be about what is happening here and now. This process is usually undertaken largely through semi-structured interviews, supported by focus groups, questionnaires, observation and previous reports where appropriate. The temptation again to jump to a quick-fix solution at this stage must be resisted by the consultant.

3. Diagnosis
The 'ideal' situation is for the client to undertake a facilitated self-diagnosis. In order to do so effectively and ensure the client is dealing with the underlying

problem, consultants have to do their own diagnosis on the basis of their data gathering. Often consultants are requested to prepare draft reports, analysing the raw data and grouping it within a framework which will make sense to the client. The reports usually take the form of using the interview statements to provide the client with a mirror to look at itself and suggesting ways to take the process forward. This presentation of the information is one of the most difficult aspects as it should ensure that the diagnosis is perceived and experienced as true by the client so the client still owns the change process.

Acceptance and Commitment
4. Gaining Acceptance and Commitment
This stage is the critical turning-point in an OD intervention. It involves ensuring that the client maintains ownership of the intervention on three levels: understanding, emotion and will. In steps two and three it is the consultant who has been gathering and analysing information but only so that s/he can then facilitate the organisation to then identify its own problems and solutions. If change is to take place, the organisation must accept the need for change and commit itself to a process for implementing it. This 'ownership' issue is often addressed through a workshop process involving all the key people concerned and using a variety of OD tools.

ODC Process Diagram

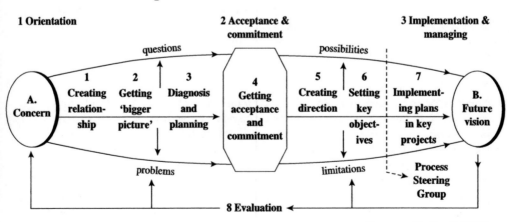

Source: D. Scott 1996

Implementing and Managing
5. Creating A Direction
In order to ensure that the momentum is not lost, a direction must be created for

the change process. This might include articulating a new mission statement, developing a statement of values or writing a revised strategic plan. The consultant may well help the client by generating a number of possible options. The difficulty at this stage is to balance the danger of the consultant overly influencing the client towards the consultant's preferred option with the importance of challenging the client not to take the easy option. At this point leadership is key, not only in providing inspiration and vision, but also in ensuring that the change process is given sufficient priority and reward.

6. Setting Key Objectives

If change is to happen, then the overall aims need to be made more specific by breaking them down into key objectives with appropriate indicators as benchmarks. Again, this process needs to be done with the involvement and commitment of all those concerned. It is sometimes useful at this stage to set up a steering group to guide and support the change project.

7. Implementing Plans

The implementation of the plans is obviously a critical activity and yet many consultants leave before anything happens. As Peter Cockman says, 'The only way you can be sure that the plan is implemented is to be there when it happens' (Cockman et al. 1992:16). The common obstacles to implementation: the client's capacity; the way it is organised; the lack of staff ownership; and the lack of leadership commitment, must be overcome. For greater effectiveness it may also be worthwhile prioritising specific projects and starting with those, developing task groups around those projects, thus ensuring wider acceptance and implementation of the changes. It is also important to know in advance how and when evaluation will occur.

8. Disengagement, Follow-Through and Evaluation

If dependency on the consultant is not to be created, there should be appropriate disengagement. On the other hand, there must be sufficient follow-through to encourage the client to maintain the implementation to the required standard. It is also important for any learning organisation to recognise the central role of reflection and evaluation in order to improve performance. Valuable lessons can be drawn from evaluations of the past change process which must inform future change activities.

The similarities between this process and three other classic OD models for organisation change are obvious.

A Comparison of Three Other Models of Change

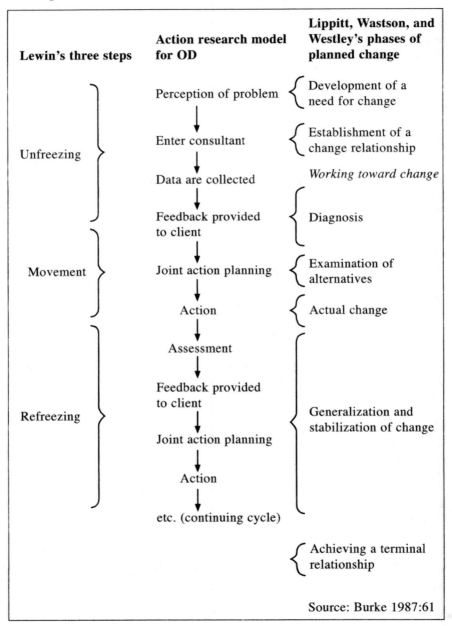

Source: Burke 1987:61

ODC METHODS

What are the Different Techniques, Tools, Instruments and Methods which ODC Uses?

Some of the problems which arise from confusion and a lack of definitions of OD can be addressed by understanding more about what sorts of intervention we are talking about when we use the term OD. One way of analysing OD interventions is by classifying them according to where the focus of the intervention is: on the individual; the team; intergroup relations or on the whole organisation.

Major Families of OD Interventions

Individual	Team	Intergroup relations	Total organisation
Life and career planning	Team-building	Intergroup activities	Strategic management planning, visioning
Coaching and counselling	Conflict resolution	Conflict resolution	Survey feedback
Education and training	Survey feedback	Survey feedback	Technostructural change
Stress management	Process consultation	Process consultation	Culture change
	HRM systems	Strategic planning activities	HRM systems development

◄─────────── Shifts in OD ──────────► Most recently ─►

As was stated in the previous chapter, there have been recent shifts in the practice of OD from a focus on interventions primarily directed inside the organisation such as group process, behavioural activities, to interventions which deal with outward elements, such as strategy and task. This reflects the increasing recognition of the importance of the external environment in organisational effectiveness. At the same time there has been a broadening of OD interventions from an almost exclusive focus on teams and intergroup relations to include interventions which either deal with the whole organisation or which recognise the critical role of individuals in top leadership positions. As can be clearly seen in the typology, some interventions affect more than one area.

Most recent of all has been the shift in focus from the single organisation to its wider environment, moving beyond even a focus on the total organisation to examining issues of inter-organisational relationships.

OD CONSULTANTS

What Roles do Consultants Play?

There are a number of different roles which a consultant may play in fostering organisational change. The success of OD consultancies is very dependent on the consultants playing the appropriate roles at the appropriate times. This requires an understanding, appreciation and experience of the different roles in order to avoid the common pitfalls of consultants playing inappropriate and confused roles. Consultants need to play roles which are appropriate and accepted by the client. The consultant 'must be very careful not to confuse being an expert on how to help an organisation learn with being an expert on the actual management problems they are trying to solve' (Schein quoted in French and Bell 1984:120).

Consultants and clients together need to analyse correctly the situation and identify and negotiate which roles are appropriate and when in order to overcome this problem and improve the effectiveness of the intervention. As Schein advises, 'if we are to be influential and genuinely helpful, we must learn how and when to be in the role of expert advice giver and when to be in the role of facilitator and catalyst' (Schein 1987:19)

Earlier in this chapter we saw that consulting roles can be divided into expert/technical approach and a more process approach. While this distinction is very useful at a simple level, the reality of consulting roles can be more complex and so it is worth exploring some of the most useful and common models.

The Lippitt and Lippitt Consulting Roles Continuum

(Lippitt and Lippitt 1979:57–75)

Most of the consulting models use Lippitt and Lippitt's classic description of consulting roles along a directive and non-directive continuum. By directive, Lippitt and Lippitt mean that the consultant assumes leadership, initiates and directs the activity. In the non-directive mode the consultant merely provides the client with data for the client to use or not. They stress that:

- these roles are not mutually exclusive and may overlap. Consultants may play a number of related roles at the same time, such as being trainer, educator and advocate;
- the consultant may play different roles with different members of the client system at the same time;
- they may change over time as the situation changes;
- consultants should have the capacity to play each of these roles;
- consultants should be able to discern which are appropriate at a particular time.

Multiple Roles of the Consultant

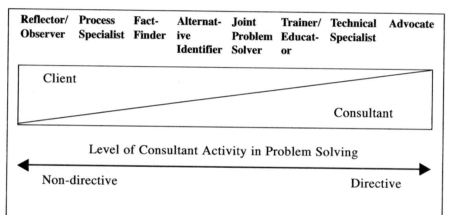

Reflector/ Observer	Process Specialist	Fact-Finder	Alternat-ive Identifier	Joint Problem Solver	Trainer/ Educat-or	Technical Specialist	Advocate

Level of Consultant Activity in Problem Solving

Non-directive   Directive

Reflector/Observer
probes, observes, mirrors and reports what is observed; retreats from active role in client decision-making.

Process Specialist
observes, diagnoses and facilitates the human dynamics and interpersonal relationships in the client system.

Fact-Finder
gathers, synthesises and analyses data relevant to the change effort.

Alternative Identifier
identifies and assesses potential alternatives.

Joint Problem Solver
offers and helps to select alternative actions needed to create the desired change

Trainer/Educator
designs, leads and evaluates learning experiences within the change effort.

Technical Specialist
proposes and guides the change effort in content or process. The client relies on the consultant's expertise.

Advocate
tries to persuade, proposes guidelines or directs the problem-solving exercise either in process or content.

The Champion, Kiel, McLendon Consulting Role Grid
(Lynton and Pareek 1992:124–130)

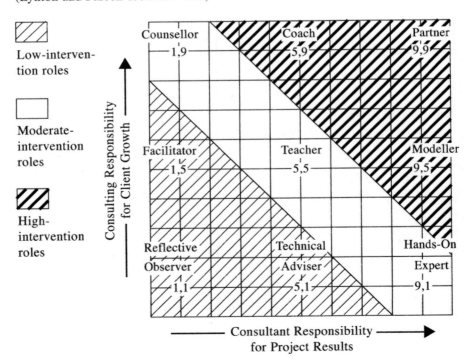

Champion, Kiel, McLendon also identify nine similar consulting roles which describe more the relationship they develop in order to collect, analyse and disseminate the information. They identify that for any consultancy the clients will have two types of need:

- the need for results – concrete outcomes, usually fairly short term and one-off;
- the need for clients to develop the capacity to solve these problems or perform new functions on a continuing basis (more akin to OD as we defined it).

They then construct a grid using consultant responsibility for results and consultant responsibility for client development as the two axes.

Hands-On Expert
the consultant undertakes the task for the client and assumes responsibility for results. The client is not expected to grow in capacity.

Modeller
assumes the client is highly responsible for project results, but that the task is carried out in a transparent way so that there is some attempt to build the capacity of the client.

Partner
the consultant has considerable responsibility, both for results and client learning. It assumes high consultant capacity in both content and process terms.

Coach
implies the consultant is not responsible for the task, but more indirectly involved in observing the client performing the task and providing feedback.

Trainer or Teacher
the consultant is even further removed from the specific task, but is concerned more with general performance.

Technical Adviser
is a back-up role of providing 'expert' advice. The consultant is moderately responsible for results but not concerned with client learning.

Counsellor
implies the consultant is almost entirely concerned with building the capacity

of the client. The counsellor constantly helps the client clarify and set goals, analyse and develop conclusions.

Facilitator
is not responsible for results but for helping the client with process-type interventions to help the client make decisions.

Reflective Observer
is a role in which the client is most responsible for both project results and for its own learning. The consultant is merely there to feed back observations and reflections.

Champion, Kiel, McLendon add the very useful dimension of the intensity of the intervention. This dimension is valuable because it shows clearly the implications of this role in terms of both consultant's time and client's (or donor's) money. By demonstrating the resource implications NGOs can avoid the problem of expecting too much from very limited consultancies. If an in-depth engagement is wanted then it has to be paid for.

Criteria for Selection of Roles

There are a number of factors which should be taken into account when identifying appropriate roles. These include:

The Client's Organisational Situation
Obviously the correct intervention roles would largely depend on the needs of the client and, closely related to that (although unfortunately not always the same), the current goals of the intervention. It would also depend on the client's capacity and whether such capacity-building was needed at all. A further influence on the client would be its own value base. For example, NGOs espousing a participative approach to development would be more likely to see the value in a more participative rather than expert consulting process. What was seen as appropriate by the client would also depend on its previous experience of consulting.

The Consultant
The consultant's competence may be the most obvious limiting factor in determining which role to play and when. In an ideal world consultants would have the experience, knowledge and confidence to play whichever role was deemed necessary, but in practice the role used is often more dependent on the consultant's personal preference, values and experience. Good OD consultants are also notoriously short of time, so the intensity of their intervention may well be lim-

ited by their availability.

Client/Consultant Relationship

An ideal client/consultant relationship is characterised by trust and openness so that there can be a collaborative determination of the appropriate client-consultant role. The reality is, however, that more often a client's unwillingness to ask for or pay for help leads to an insufficient consulting role; or that the consultant's need to see personal results leads to an unhealthy creation of dependence. In addition, during the first contact between consultant and client the importance of getting the job done is often stressed and therefore a more directive role for consultants is requested and delivered. Over time this role may become more facilitative and less directive as trust and credibility is built up. The bottom line which often determines the role played in interventions is the nature of the contract.

What Styles do OD Consultants Need to Use?

As well as playing different roles, the interviews with OD consultants in Africa revealed that consultants had to use different styles. Consultant styles can be defined as the behaviours consultants adopt in interactions with clients. Most consultants have a particular style they are most comfortable with, but, as with consulting roles, no one style will be effective in all situations. Consultants often have to adopt different styles at different times, even with the same client at different phases of the consulting cycle (this is an obvious advantage of using teams of consultants) Cockman et al. (1992) use Blake and Mouton's descriptions to identify four distinct, legitimate and comprehensive intervention styles.

Prescriptive style

Perhaps the most common consulting style, a prescriptive approach implies that a consultant listens to the client's problem, collects and analyses the data needed and presents the client with a set of recommendations. It is quite similar to the 'expert' or 'doctor–patient' models. This style is very popular as it offers deceptively appealing quick-fix solutions and allows consultants to be viewed (and view themselves) and paid as experts. Because the client is largely passive, it does not allow much opportunity for client development or growth and may well create an unhealthy dependence.

There are situations where it is an appropriate approach, sometimes with nuts-and-bolts organisational issues or severe crises where time is very limited.

Catalytic style

This helps clients to gather more information about the issue, analyse it and make a diagnosis of the root cause(s) of the problem. The solution to these problems is always generated by the client. This diagnostic style may involve many different data-gathering methodologies, but may also may simply be helping clients make sense of already existing data using techniques such as force-field analysis or problem trees. It assumes that the client already possesses the relevant data. It is a very versatile approach which can be used in may phases of the consulting process, though it runs the risk of unconsciously slipping into prescription.

Confrontational style

At times consultants may need to confront an organisation or a leadership with discrepancies between espoused values and actual behaviours or to point out the implications of carrying through certain actions. Confrontation is often needed in the common scenario when the person (or group) recruiting the consultant is part of the problem, but has assumed that the cause lies entirely outside. The aim is to highlight the discrepancy and give the client an opportunity to address it if they wish.

The confrontational style assumes that clients are able to do something about the problem. It is usually a short-term style employed from a firm base of trust and therefore usually not until later stages of an intervention. It may generate an emotional response which needs to be carefully handled (either by the consultant) or another member of the consultancy team

Acceptant style

This stresses the value of empathetic listening, and providing emotional support. 'Neutral non-judgmental support can help clients relax their defences, confront disabling emotional reactions and find their own way forward' (Cockman et al. 1992:23). This is typical of the early stages of counselling.

In order to implement this style effectively, consultants need to be able to 'wear other peoples' moccasins'. This style recognises the importance of dealing with the very real emotional reactions to organisational issues rather than merely assuming all human reactions will be rational. In situations where the NGO's context is rapidly changing, people need to be helped to come to terms with the resulting losses (in terms of redundant programmes, skills, roles for example). It is also frequently needed in helping NGO founders adjust to the common crisis of leadership when the organisation develops past its pioneer phase.

These styles need to be consciously chosen as different ones will be needed at different times.

What Skills do OD Consultants Need?

In order to play these roles effectively and choose appropriate styles, consultants need considerable skills and abilities. While it might appear unhelpful to construct a too idealistic wish list or a false exercise to try to separate and dis-aggregate these skills from the whole person, it is clear that there are a number of abilities consultants should possess to be most effective, and it is often only by recognising deficiencies that they can be addressed. CORAT and INTRAC developed a comprehensive checklist for developing consultants skills during their joint practice covering issues of:

- personal management and awareness;
- cross-cultural awareness;
- inter-personal communication skills;
- facilitation and enabling skills;
- working as an agent of change;
- understanding how organisations work and develop;
- contracting;
- team-working;
- data collection;
- sensing and diagnosing;
- intervening;
- evaluation and closure.

What are the Characteristics of Good OD Consultants?

The qualities needed to be an effective OD consultant are severely underestimated by Northern and Southern NGOs alike. As a result, in response to the increased demand we are witnessing the explosive growth of people calling themselves OD consultants. Uncovering sensitive issues at the heart of organisations' cultures can unleash very powerful forces and there is the potential to do massive harm to an organisation if it is not handled properly. Donors, clients and consultants must pay more attention to the characteristics of good OD consultants if they are to avoid doing more harm than good.

NGOs need to beware of consultants who offer off-the-shelf expert solutions to unique organisational issues.

In OD Debate Vol. 2 No. 5 (Oct. 1995) a number of top NGO OD consultants in South Africa offered their opinions on 'What does it take to be an OD practitioner'.

Some of the main personal characteristics offered were:

- Organisational experience – 'a fair amount of life and organisational

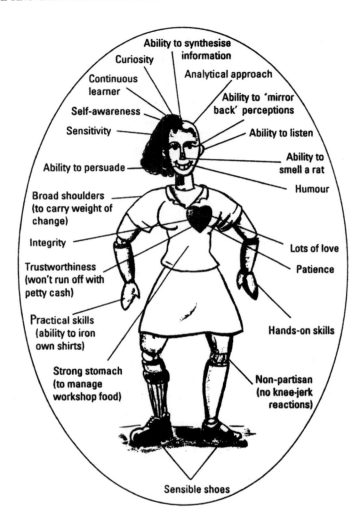

Ability to synthesise information
Curiosity
Continuous learner
Analytical approach
Self-awareness
Ability to 'mirror back' perceptions
Sensitivity
Ability to listen
Ability to persuade
Ability to smell a rat
Humour
Broad shoulders (to carry weight of change)
Integrity
Lots of love
Trustworthiness (won't run off with petty cash)
Patience
Practical skills (ability to iron own shirts)
Hands-on skills
Strong stomach (to manage workshop food)
Non-partisan (no knee-jerk reactions)
Sensible shoes

experience enables good OD'. According to the World Bank the reality is that, 'consulting firms and individual consultants (as organisational outsiders) often lack direct operational experience' (Buyck 1991:91). The growth of independent consultants may also be a symptom of people who are unable or unwilling to subject themselves to the pressures of working within organisations and yet are very willing to advise others on how to do it!

- 'A curious and continuous learner'.

- A high degree of self-knowledge. As Kisare says, 'when the dangers are so much more subtle and hidden than in most other professions, the practitioner must remain ever alert to the chance of being ambushed by the contradictions and the only real defence is supreme self-awareness' (1996:3). It is important for consultants to have a strong knowledge of who they are, and what values, biases and insecurities they bring to a client. It is also vital that they are aware of their limitations and are able to ask for outside help when they need it and simply respond, 'I do not know'.

- Confidence and an ability to work without being controlled by one's own needs for recognition and positive feedback.

- Sensitivity to power dynamics within organisations and an ability to handle conflict as well as recognising one's own power in the situation.

- Patience, understanding, and an ability to observe and listen to the problems of the client. When a consultant enters a client system there is so much that s/he does not know – unless the consultant is able to listen actively, the tendency will be to fit the client into a convenient pigeon-hole. A good OD practitioner is said to travel light with her or his greatest asset being the ability to listen or facilitate.

- Both facilitation skills and a facilitative attitude. These skills 'are labelled as soft but are the most difficult, demanding and challenging skills to master' (Kaplan and Taylor 1996:7). This should also be coupled with an ability to persuade (as OD specialists do not have the authority to implement change). They need to have the political skills to create the acceptance and commitment to move the change forward.

- An analytic approach and possession of good judgement. Consultants need also to be able to live without providing easy answers and be able to tolerate ambiguity and paradox – holding sometimes conflicting truths in creative tension rather than seeking a compromise between the two.

- A thorough knowledge of organisations, being well-schooled in different approaches and with the competence to use a variety of OD tools.

- A knowledge of what is happening in the environment of the organisation.

- Strong values and commitment of the OD consultant are seen to be as important as the content and process of the OD intervention itself. As Allan

Kaplan says, 'if there is no love then more harm can be done than good' (1995:5). Humility is also key, avoiding consultant tendencies towards narcissism!

Esper (1990:287) notes other competencies of the consultant in relation to the client which include:

- an ability to develop rapport and trust with the client;

- an empathy and sensitivity to see the world from the client's eyes;

- an ability to give feedback 'side by side';

- a 'gutsiness' to 'speak the unspeakable' and to take tough stands, balanced with a sense of timing.

As Dave Harding says,

> above all look for those OD practitioners who confess to doubts and holes in their understanding of organisations, who say they will learn with you when they work with you, who believe there are usually no quick fix answers but rather a need to spend as long as it takes – and to go as slowly as is needed. (1995:4)

Part Two

The Practice of OD Consultancy with NGOs in Africa

Chapter 3

OD Case Studies

My conclusion is that there is a vast gap between OD as researched and written down and OD as actually practised. Weisbord quoted in McLean et al. 1982:86

INTRODUCTION

It is important to learn as much as we can from the theory of OD, while recognising that the real world does not always conform to our theoretical boxes and frameworks. To help NGOs take considered and appropriate decisions about the use of OD consultancy as a capacity-building intervention, it is critical that actual experience is analysed and lessons learnt and applied from that experience. These cases provide in graphic and practical terms what OD consultancy looks like in NGO reality; what it can achieve; what it cannot achieve; where it works well; where it does not work so well; and how it can be measured and managed.

Eastern and Southern Africa was chosen as the geographic focus of the research because these countries have the most established providers of ODC to NGOs (other than India) and therefore experience on which to base the findings.

Nine case studies have been written by OD consultants, most of whom are from Africa. The institutions and individuals which provided case studies are:

CDRA	(Lynette Maart, James Taylor – South Africa)
Olive	(Carol-Ann Foulis – South Africa)
CORAT	(William Ogara – Kenya)
Matrix	(Daudi Waithaka – Kenya)
EASUN	(Mosi Kisare – Tanzania)
David Harding	(UK)
INTRAC	(Rick James and Liz Goold – UK)

The consultants were selected on the basis of their recognised involvement in OD consultancies with NGOs. The case studies document the consultants' experience of one particular intervention they were involved with. The cases cover a broad range of countries including: South Africa; Namibia; Malawi; Tanzania; Kenya and Eritrea, revealing the importance of the context. The cases describe a variety of different interventions, some of which lasted only a few weeks while others have been ongoing for more than three years. They illustrate different styles and approaches of consultants.

The cases do have sufficient commonality to be able to draw out key issues and success factors in Part 3 of the book and be able to conclude with the implications for Northern NGOs' support of OD consultancy in Part 4.

USING EVALUATIONS AS AN OD TOOL?!

A Fellowship of Churches in South Africa

James Taylor (CDRA)

Introduction

Evaluations, once the *bete noire* of 'developmental' advocates are increasingly being used as an opportunity for NGOs to take stock and review triggering very 'developmental' OD interventions.

In 1995 a Durban-based 'Fellowship of Churches and Christian Organisations' requested CDRA (a noted OD provider from Cape Town) to help them undertake an evaluation. This complemented a previous intervention from CDRA with one particular programme.

While the evaluation was part of a regular six-yearly evaluation process, the intervention had been brought forward by two years because of the profound changes that had taken place in South Africa with the accompanying dramatically accelerated rate of change and political violence in KwaZulu Natal. Added to this external change, the NGO itself had just merged with another organisation.

The main activities of the NGO were:

- Peace-making and peace-building;
- Education for democracy;
- Development and reconstruction.

The Aim of the Intervention

After the initial request was received, a short process of refining and clarifying the terms of reference took place between CDRA and the organisation's director (together with a small group of mandated staff).

The intervention aimed to:

- review the NGO's present context and explore likely future changes which could affect the organisation;

- revisit the statement of the organisation's fundamental mission and purpose and amend if necessary;

- identify the most critical areas in which the NGO needed to undergo change;

- identify the individuals, mechanisms and structures through which the processes of change were to be planned and managed.

The NGO put together a team of three consultants from different organisations in order to access specialist input in relation to the particular socio/political context and the church context as well as the OD expertise of the team leader.

The next step was to negotiate a detailed contract which included: the objectives; the process; the schedule including dates; responsibilities of the client organisation; and estimated cost of the intervention.

As the client organisation had a firmly established commitment to regular evaluation which was costed into its budgets, it made absolutely no sense to the consultant that donors were in any way directly involved in the process. It was always clear that the process was wholly owned and commissioned by the organisation itself.

The Implementation Process

The implementation process incorporated the following components:

1. An environmental scan conducted by a member of the evaluation team in the form of a workshop and written up as a short report.

2. Interviews with major stakeholders including representatives of member churches, recipients of service and staff. In all 42 interviews were conduct ed

3. A facilitated organisational workshop with those directly involved in making operational the overall aims and objectives of the organisation. All the staff actively engaged with the findings of the evaluation and used it to inform a strategic planning process of their own. The final product then became the action plan related to changes identified as being necessary and relevant by the organisation itself, rather than the recommendations of the consultants.

4. The last step was the compilation and presentation of the final report. The final report was presented to a meeting of the full board and many of the staff of the organisation.

Closure and Next Steps

The process effectively ended with the presentation of the final report as stipulated in the contract, but the relationship with the client organisation is seen as ongoing, and there has been occasional contact around specific organisational issues. From the consultant's point of view it is up to the client to initiate any specific request for assistance in the future.

Preliminary Assessment of the Impact
Recent interviews 18 months after the event with a cross-section of staff revealed a very positive impact in many ways:

Very Existence and Survival
Respondents within the NGO were very clear that *'if this organisation had not seriously thought through its core purpose it could have been on the way to its demise'* and that without the intervention *'there was no way we could sustain it the way we were going.'*

Ability to Take on Its Own Change Process
At the very heart of ODC is facilitating the NGO to take charge of its own development. Not only has the organisation *'set in motion all the recommendations from the process except for salary structures which we will do in the first half of this year'*, but also they are still consciously working on the outcomes more than a year later. In addition, one of the other case studies in the research ('The Independence of CRCs' by Olive) describes in more detail how the NGO took on one of the recommendations and used another provider to carry out an OD process with just one part of the Fellowship of Churches.

Changes in Organisational Capacity
• Identity, Vision and Mission
The process also led to very real changes in organisational capacity. In the words of the client, *'it led to us looking very deeply at what we are trying to do. We emerged from the evaluation with the clearest conception of what we are about'* and *'the process gave us greater understanding of what we are doing and why'*. The client asserted that *'the workshop led to a real paradigm shift'* and the NGO even has a new mission statement reflecting that shift.

• Strategy
The OD intervention resulted in very real changes in strategy with programmes being closed down *'which did not make us very popular'*.

• Structures and Systems
Structural changes are often the easiest changes to notice. As a result of the intervention the NGO did create some new full time posts for finance.

Furthermore, community committees were strengthened and management committees introduced. Clear roles and responsibilities were also developed which for more than one person *'eased the load on me as tasks were delegated and my load was spread. It was too much for me to be effective'*.

- People

This OD consultancy also brought significant changes in 'people' related areas. At the level of leadership, *'it saved the director from burn-out'* and for staff there were considerable changes in motivation, for *'if people understand how their work fits with the overall objectives of the organisation, then massive energy is released'*.

Changes at Community Level

At a community level, there are visible changes too, although more indirect than at an organisational level, as *'change has a ripple effect outwards'*.

If an organisation is suffering from severe organisational problems then this will be a significant constraint on their effectiveness. *'Our staff were overstretched and stressed and not performing optimally'* ... *'We were involved in superficial diffuse engagements which led to staff dissatisfaction and failure to reach their potential'*. Addressing these organisational ills will have a very real effect at the grass-roots level with one staff member stating that, *'we are no longer just crisis driven. It has become more proactive. I strongly believe that this has an impact on the beneficiaries'*.

Certainly the OD engagement did have a direct impact in terms of the programme methodologies with the *'communities involved in the planning process for first time'*.

INDEPENDENCE DAY?

The Independence of 'Community Resource Centres' from the Fellowship of Churches in South Africa

Carol-Ann Foulis (Olive)

Introduction

Olive (OD & Training) first began working with the client in February 1995, when it was contracted to write job descriptions and develop a payment framework for Community Resource Centres (CRCs). The CRC Programme comprises 14 centres which are all situated within the greater Durban area and provide the following services: paralegal advice, community development, lobbying and networking. There are 28 staff employed by the programme who are paid by the 'parent' organisation. Managerial and administrative support also comes from the parent organisation which is the same Durban-based Fellowship of Churches mentioned in the previous case study. In fact dealing with some of the human resource systems issues and structural issues was one of the recommendations of the previous OD intervention by CDRA.

The Aim of the Intervention

The initial request to look at job descriptions and a payment framework for the centres was based largely on the CDRA work. Furthermore, the importance of the CRCs becoming (more) independent of the organisations within which they are located, as well as the need to increase their sustainability were also strongly emphasised. These recommendations have subsequently been translated into what has become known as the 'independence process' – a long-term process of change which has had to be planned and embarked upon in an integrated, holistic way.

While Olive initially contracted with the client around the delivery of a specific product – job descriptions and a payment framework, the Director also wanted the work to 'test' staff's understanding of and readiness to move towards independence. This HR request also set the ball rolling for the OD intervention.

Shifting from HR to OD

Having delivered the product of job descriptions and a payment framework as per the initial brief, in August 1995, Olive then entered into a new contract with the client which had as its longer-term goal the increased independence of the CRCs from the parent organisation.

The Intervention Process

The intervention process can be divided into three phases: each with its own objectives.

Phase 1: Creating a vision of independence

The first phase was marked by the appointment of four Zonal Co-ordinators to assist the centres in their move to independence. The objectives were as follows:

1. Consultations with the client to explore ideas and share views to develop an understanding of the client's vision of independence.

2. Workshops with staff to assist people in understanding what would be involved in the change process; providing opportunities for people to share their views, feelings, concerns and challenges about independence.

3. Training and support of Zonal Co-ordinators in the transition from staff member to Zonal Co-ordinator and equipping them with the skills required for their new position, such as planning, supervision, delegation and time management.

Phase 2: Review period and adapted contract

A review was conducted in June 1996 to assess the extent to which intended outcomes had been achieved in each of the three areas. Based on this review, the consultant entered into an adapted contract with the client which had as its key objective the training and development of the Zonal Co-ordinators (in recognition of their key role in the change process). Another feature of this phase was the establishment of clearer boundaries regarding the consultant's role in the change process.

At this stage, it was decided that Olive would no longer play a role in the general training of programme staff. It was felt that staff were sufficiently oriented to the idea of independence and that the organisation itself needed to drive the next stage in this process.

It was also agreed that the consultant would not be involved in the training and development of local committees. While this was clearly an important component of the next phase, it was acknowledged that this was outside of the consultant's organisational mission and area of 'expertise'. Other organisations were referred to who could assist in this area.

Phase 3: The way ahead

From December 1996, the relationship between the client and consultant enters into yet another phase. This is in part because certain objectives have been achieved, and also because new circumstances are calling for new kinds of support and approaches to the change process. At this point in time, the content of this phase is undefined.

Factors Constraining the Process

A number of factors have hindered or slowed down the process:

- The style of the Programme Manager has reinforced a particular way of relating to people which the independence process is seeking to change. Given that the Programme Manager is the pioneer and possibly stands to lose too much from the change, it has been important for the consultant not to skirt around these issues but to find ways of dealing with them directly and constructively.

- To a large extent, there is no external imperative for change. The parent organisation has initiated the independence of the CRCs and the deadlines by which change needs to take place are variable and extend considerably far into the future. This has its advantages, but the lack of urgency and need to change has sometimes resulted in a level of complacency which has curtailed the action that needs to be taken.

- The level of management and administrative experience of staff of the CRC Programme is limited in certain respects. Many staff members have worked only for this particular programme and do not have other organisational experience to draw on. This is significant given that management and administrative skills are needed for an independent CRC. The change process is therefore slow as time needs to be spent building the capacity of staff in these areas.

Factors Promoting the Process

Many factors have helped or been important in taking the process forward:

- The appointment and training of the Zonal Co-ordinators, with an increasing emphasis on their role as key change agents, has given a sense of urgency, importance and focus to the independence process. They have been a tangible sign, particularly to staff, that this process is 'for real'.

- The appointment of a temporary 'Programme Co-ordinator' with a very participative style of management, while the Programme Manager has been on sabbatical, has significantly facilitated the move towards independence. The consultant has noticed increased energy, enthusiasm and interest amongst staff which seems to be related to this person coming into the organisation.

- Having dedicated capacity for managing the change process has been particularly important. It has been the responsibility of the 'Programme Co-ordinator' to focus on the independence process.

- The recent introduction of the client to different models of 'independence' has provided the client with an opportunity to learn from others' experiences.

- Olive has used a team for this intervention, rather than one consultant. This has been particularly useful in ensuring that our approach remains open, innovative, critically reflective and professional. Furthermore, keeping the same people part of this team has had a number of advantages, particularly for understanding the complexity and dynamics of the intervention.

- From the start and throughout the intervention, the method of diagnosing the system and making recommendations was a highly interactive process. The consultant did not offer a neatly mapped out path for independence of the centres. As *'staff were involved throughout the process ... involved in developing and negotiating the ToR.'* this meant that staff very much owned the change process.

- The quality of the reporting was also seen by CRC staff as being important. *'The detailed report with key questions to address in the workshop was very helpful. Their reports were thorough and accessible, prompt and with clear recommendations and conclusions'.*

- It was important for Olive to regularly define and review its role in the OD process and to set specific objectives in relation to this role as it became difficult to maintain the different roles and responsibilities of the client versus those of the consultant at certain times. Given the importance of ensuring that ownership of the process remained with the client, the consultants made considerable efforts to continually clarify their role – *'we were beginning to drive the process. Because they were too busy we would be bringing more of the ideas and setting the agendas ... so we said ... we will leave it to you to contact us. They brought proposals and we formalised them into briefs'.*

Preliminary Assessment of the Impact

It is difficult at this stage to measure the impact of the intervention because Olive's relationship with the client continues. However, the process has been monitored along the way and a number of goals (both planned and unplanned) have been achieved. The impressions of both client and consultant have also been regularly gathered and reflected upon. The consultant has encouraged the client to establish its own criteria for measuring the impact and using its own means for collecting this information.

Some of the impressions of the key achievements to date are:

- People are clearer on what is needed for an independent organisation and are in the process of formulating plans which will indicate how they will go about achieving this. There is a vision for what will be achieved.

- Staff (and some of the local committee members) have had opportunities to raise their fears, concerns and questions about the independence process and the parent organisation has responded to these. To some extent, this has built a critical mass of people who understand, support and drive this move to independence. Furthermore, the parent organisation has realised the importance of letting go.

- The attitudes and behaviour of certain staff members have changed in the time that the consultant has been working with them. Staff are behaving in a more *'responsible'* manner.

- The growth and development of the Zonal Co-ordinators is also significant. They have received training in a number of areas and are also behaving in a more responsible, independent manner. The management has noted *'a lot more confidence amongst the zonal coordinators'* with them *'taking more initiative, greater participation in management meetings and deeper issues raised, delegation of responsibility coped with'*.

- A number of structural changes have occurred as a result of this intervention. First, the appointment of the Zonal Co-ordinators has played an important role in moving some of the control and power away from the parent organisation to the CRCs. Secondly, it is likely that the post of Programme Co-ordinator will remain as a dedicated internal resource for managing the change process.

The change that is required in this process is enormous – it is about moving the CRCs from a state of financial, administrative and management dependence for the last 14 years to one of independence. Furthermore, being independent brings with it a set of challenges for which some people are not and may never be ready. However, the consultant acknowledges that change is a series of steps that need to be managed and be made manageable. They also need to be heading in an agreed to direction. What the consultants have done *'is walk with the client for some distance along the path of change'*. Getting the client on this path and assisting the different components in becoming skilled, aligned and ready for change has been a lengthy but productive process.

ARISING FROM THE ASHES?

Arusha Beekeepers Association

Mosi Kisare (EASUN)

Introduction

The Arusha Beekeepers Association (ABA) is a large, but fragile NGO. Started in 1991, it has been involved primarily in providing training to its 1800 members, spread throughout a large geographic area. ABA has no full-time staff, but has relied on a voluntary coordinator as well as the Government extension workers. In late 1994 problems arose in the implementation of a Danish-funded training programme; internal arguments broke out over the leadership and distribution of resources. An acrimonious split ensued and a rival association was set up.

Around the same time, one of ABA's main projects came to an end and a report was sent to the donor. The donor realised that there were significant problems within the organisation and suggested ABA approach EASUN. At this stage ABA had little idea of what EASUN was and admitted that *'if the donor had never mentioned EASUN we would not have dared contact them'*.

In response, EASUN consultants met with ABA to seek further clarification on the expectations of ABA, their understanding of EASUN and its approach to organisational capacity-building. It became clear that ABA had no prior exposure to the concept of OD. According to the director, *'in the beginning we had no idea what OD was. When the donor advised us to go and see EASUN, we thought they would do an audit on us. At that stage we were very defensive and conflictive'*.

While the intervention had been suggested by the donor and finance for it offered, EASUN proceeded to dialogue with ABA rather than the donor. Two OD consultancy contracts were drawn between ABA and EASUN to clarify the process.

The Aim of the Intervention

- The expected outcomes of the intervention included:
- a more focused mission statement;
- streamlined members' expectations;
- restructured governance and operational relations;
- improved functional relationships in the operational structure;
- a framework for action-planning;
- indicators of goal achievement.

The Implementation Process

The intervention involved two main phases, with considerable contact in between.

The first workshop in April 1995 was held with 20 members of ABA, including the management, extension agents, Council members and members' representatives. The workshop examined the main problems facing ABA.

The initial politeness in the workshop soon gave way to bitter criticism of the coordinator with accusations (in his own words) of being 'a dictator, a thief and even threats of lawsuits'. The consultant had to spend significant time with the coordinator in a counselling mode in order to help him deal with and come to terms with the resulting defensiveness and conflict.

The consultant also had to lead the rest of the group into more constructive ways of dealing with the issues. This was done partly through participants listing some broad themes to focus upon in assessing ABA, and developing a role-play which simulated a meeting of various stakeholders to design a Terms of Reference for an evaluation of ABA. The role play surfaced and sharpened critical issues of mission and strategy in a less conflictive manner.

Between the workshops, there was regular contact between the consultant and both the coordinator and chairman of ABA. These meetings were mainly about further planning or clarification of issues, but also some further individual counselling on the necessary leadership approach to a membership organisation riven by conflict.

The second phase in January 1996 entailed another short workshop assisting ABA to examine a potential new role and strategy in relation to its abilities and the expectations of its members. The main diagnostic tools used were an environmental scan, small group discussions and role-play and change scenarios. The outcome of this second workshop was a decision by ABA to discontinue its previous role of being a large umbrella body for thousands of members and instead to concentrate on playing a facilitation role in helping smaller grassroots groups of beekeepers to emerge.

While the main interventions were only two short three-day workshops, there was considerable time spent in between on planning and counselling. It is therefore safe to speak of one full year of ongoing engagement with the process.

Factors Promoting the Process

The fact that ABA were on the brink of collapse and in danger of imminent death gave them great ownership of the need to change. They were also prepared to take a hard honest look at themselves in making that change. In addition, the coordinator had a significant interest in fostering change as he wanted to maintain (or regain as he had been unofficially sacked!) his position in the organisation.

The consultant quickly established the necessary level of trust and rapport and developed a participative process which used much role-play and encouraged members to ask questions of themselves. The effectiveness of the consultancy was undoubtedly also helped by the fascination and enthusiasm of the ABA's coordinator for the participative OD process itself.

ABA also invested themselves in the process, *'we paid for all the OD meetings including providing transport and food for all the members. We also had to pay the consultants a fee. Even this token amount made us feel more responsible for the intervention and value it more'*.

Factors Constraining the Process

The workshop process, however, was constrained by poor organisation; the spillover of the internal organisational tensions which needed to be addressed from time to time; and the previous problems of communication which meant the coordinator was continually called aside by members to clear up matters relating to their dues.

Other constraints in the process itself included communication difficulties which hindered a free flow between participants and the facilitators (despite the fact that they were the same nationality!). There were two levels of frustration: on the one hand, the impression of the participants that they would have benefited more if the consultant was a Kiswahili expert and, on the other, by the consultant's recognition that effective communication here did require a profound interpretation of foreign cultural imagery and metaphor.

There was also the problem of some members of the Executive Committee wanting to cast the consultants in the expert role, abdicating to them responsibility for recommendations of ways forward *'they were to work on our workshop ideas as "experts" and come up with their recommendations'*.

Preliminary Assessment of the Impact

Very little seems to have been implemented since the last intervention over 18 months ago and there has been little discernible impact at the level of beneficiaries. Members of the board comment that while *'the intervention of EASUN was great, the implementation since has been poor'*.

This raises the inherent dilemma of every consultancy intervention – the main factor determining its success is out of the consultant's hands. Consultants can certainly encourage and help the implementation process but the whole OD approach implies that the NGO must take responsibility for its own development and change itself. Most OD practitioners are very aware of the dangers of fostering dependency on the consultant by playing too great a role at the implementation stage. As the EASUN consultant said 'it was important for ABA to struggle on their own at this stage'.

So on the one hand it should be noted that *'the effect (and dynamism) of the OD process can be lost if not implemented quickly',* but on the other, outsiders tend to have a much shorter time-scale for seeing results and may need to take into account that a consultative OD process in a membership organisation covering a vast area will necessarily take a long time. It can be argued that 'impact is in the eyes of the beholder'. Certainly the ABA leadership feel that the OD process was successful, *'without the OD process right now we wouldn't be standing – we would not exist'.* They feel it has also contributed to a significant development of ABA's identity, *'most importantly it made us know ourselves and our responsibilities. Before we never knew what we were doing and why'.* The OD process also helped deal with the considerable internal conflict in a positive manner as it *'developed our members'* participation in the organisation' and, perhaps even more significantly, radically altered the attitude and behaviour of the leadership.

Whether this intervention is deemed successful in the end will depend on whether the impact is felt at the beneficiary level. At the moment the process has enabled only ABA to die to its old self, allowing the potential for something new and better to arise from the ashes. While some members claim that even if ABA is never resurrected, the OD process can be deemed a success as *'the individual learning ... hopes and ideas remain. The idea of facilitating the development of small bee-keeping groups will not die, even if ABA as an organisation does'.* Others, including most donors, would probably take a harder stance, measuring success in the implementation of those ideas, not just in the existence of the ideas.

DIOCESAN DEVELOPMENT

OD Within the Wider Church Context

The Diocese of Sende

Liz Goold and *William Ogara*

Introduction

The Diocese of Sende has been in existence since 1959. It covers a vast expanse of land in Southern Africa which is largely inhabited by pastoralists. The present bishop has been there since its inception 38 years ago, but will be retiring in the near future. From the beginning, the diocese adopted a decentralised approach towards development with a large community development project in one part of the diocese and a diocesan development education programme based in a parish. Both were only loosely attached to the development office (DO) of the diocese. Other sector programmes emerged as departments as funding allowed with the development office playing a coordination role. Meanwhile, priests (largely foreigners) accessed funds from external sources for their own individual parish development projects.

The Trigger and False Start

Development initiatives fluctuated over the years and there was a high turnover of staff in the development office. The Development Education Programme split off from the diocese in the early 1990s. At this time, there were a series of evaluations and rejected donor proposals which raised questions about the role, direction and sustainability of the development coordination office. With the impending departure of the bishop, funding looking more precarious, and the loss of implementation role for the DO, a crisis was brewing. One major donor (75%) suggested that the diocese undertake a feasibility study for future work and identified a firm which had been started primarily by some university lecturers in their spare time. This consultancy proved disastrous with all the stakeholders quickly feeling confused and alienated. When the consultancy firm threatened legal action if they were not allowed to finish the work, the diocese was finally forced to think through the purpose of the consultancy and whether they wanted one at all.

The diocese decided that it did have some internal weaknesses which needed addressing and that it needed to have donors (and these donors were requiring it) so 'why not dialogue to see how we can benefit from the process?'. They allowed the first consultancy to finish and *'swept the report under the carpet'*.

The main donor realised that the first choice of consultants had been a mistake and provided a bridging grant for the diocese to submit a new proposal. The donor encouraged the Bishop to approach a local consultancy organisation which focused on providing organisational support to church-related organisations in Africa and had an ongoing relationship with a UK-based NGO consultancy (which was invited to join them at certain stages in the process).

The Intervention Process
Initial Meetings

Initial meetings were held between the consultants, the Bishop, the Development Office (DO) staff and others in the diocese to establish trust and rapport and highlight the key issues, which included:

- the development officer did not have a background or experience in development;
- there was pressure from the donor to produce a clear mission, priorities, plan and budget;
- the DO was very dependent on the goodwill of priests and many priests saw the DO as marginal and only there to access funds for their projects;
- the missionary priests were still influential. Their prime accountability was to their order/congregation/own donors rather than the diocese;
- with the departure of the DEP programme the DO was largely a coordinator of projects and programmes without any clarity of its own role and identity;
- given the weakness of the DO, the wider diocese could not be ignored in any change process.

Broadening the Consultation

To address the wider issues identified, the consultants saw the need to broaden the initial diagnosis and a 3-day workshop was held, which included a historical review of the diocese identifying significant changes and events up to the present day, stakeholder analysis, an assessment of the culture and life stage of the diocese and the DO and an analysis of the strengths and constraints of the DO. From this analysis, some of the initial diagnosis was confirmed, particularly that the needs were inextricably linked to the wider diocese. The separation between the pastoral and developmental work of the church was seen to be artificial and potentially damaging.

Diocesan Meetings

An already existing meeting of the Diocesan Pastoral Council (DPC), which brought together lay representatives from parishes, clergy and women's and youth groups in the diocese was used to take the process further. The council, including the bishop, agreed to continue with a process of forming a shared vision for the diocese. A representative planning team was given a mandate to plan this process, with the support of the consultants who sat in as observers at this meeting. A gradual shift was taking place, moving this from a DO initiative into a diocesan one.

Contracting

The development coordinator was part of the planning team in his role as secretary to the diocesan pastoral council. With the endorsement of the planning team, he wrote a proposal to the main donor to pay for this capacity-building process. A clear contract was agreed with the consultants. The main donor expected that within the year the DO should present a vision, as well as a concrete programme with measurable objectives, and activities for a 3–4 year period.

The Process Used

Questionnaire

To ensure that the process was as participative as possible, a simple questionnaire relating to past changes and dreams for the future was sent to all parishes, and representatives were nominated to be part of a diocesan-wide consultation.

Vision and Mission Workshop

Over 50 people took part from nearly every parish. The majority were lay. The Bishop was unable to attend as he was on leave. This consultation gave particular emphasis to the changes occurring external and internal to the diocese, undertaking an in-depth social analysis of the country. Different group's perceptions were openly shared, along with the church's social teachings, and the Bishop's Pastoral letters. From this, participants were encouraged to dream of a future vision for the diocese and how the diocese would contribute towards this. Discussions and debates went on late into the night. Those who were, at first, resistant – particularly one or two influential priests – began to change their approach and engage actively with the process.

After four days, a draft vision and mission statement was agreed upon by the entire group. Ideas were also put forward for ways of ensuring this vision and mission was shared and owned throughout the diocese as concerns were raised about the small number of priests having gone through this experience and their possible resistance later.

Donor Demands

Meanwhile, the main donor requested that a detailed programme for the following year be submitted in the next two months by the DO together with a consolidated budget. During a visit by the main donor, open and frank discussions took place with the Bishop about changes occurring in the donor world and the need for change. They also expressed their specific concerns about the competence of the development coordinator saying that *'without skilled people we will not be attracted to fund you in the future'*. These suggestions were resisted by the Bishop who felt that the donor was dictating what should emerge from this process rather than letting it evolve from and be managed from within. The donor, in turn, felt that the Bishop did not fully appreciate the urgency and need for change.

The African Synod – Bringing the Priests on Board
The central role of priests at parish level meant that they had to be brought on board. To overcome their initial resistance, the Bishop invited all priests to arrive one day early before their annual meeting to give some time to the vision process.

After considerable discussion most of the priests supported the draft vision and mission statements, though some challenged its theological basis as it was put together largely by lay people. Further discussion was desired. Those priests who had been involved in the diocesan consultation spoke up and played an active role in winning some of their fellow priests around. The consultants' understanding of the church set-up also helped in this respect.

There was a general agreement that pastoral debates within the African Synod on issues such as inculturation, communication, justice and peace needed to be integrated into this OD process. Since then there has been a consolidation of these suggestions. The planning teams for both processes have merged and have begun to work on a statement of core values as well as strategies. The vision and mission proposal has now been embraced and endorsed.

WHAT HAPPENS NEXT

This OD process is still ongoing and according to the client may continue for another two years (though the role of the consultant may change in this time).

Preliminary Assessment of the Impact
While the process is still mid-way and the translation of verbal commitments into practice will take time, the client identified significant changes which had taken place already in terms of:

Wider Church Diocese
A clearer and shared identity: *'We have managed to come up with clear dioce-*

san *vision and mission'* and by *'harmonising the African Synod debates with the OD process'* they have overcome dualism to some degree and separation of spiritual and secular.

The process is also contributing to the 'indigenisation of the church'. The vision and direction of African lay people and priests has been endorsed by the church. In this way the process is having a much wider impact on the church as a whole.

Development Office
The DO has also progressed in its:

Identity: *'we now know what we are doing, why and what we are going to do'.*
Strategy: *'helped with a better focus for development activities'.*
Systems: *'we are in the process of standardising our financial systems and manual'.*
Programming: *'Now we are sure the demands come from the people'.*

According to church members, these changes have had a direct impact on beneficiaries.

Beneficiaries
There has been a change in attitude with people taking responsibility for their own their own development: *'taking initiative themselves and no longer waiting for handouts'.*

More broadly the process has had an impact on the wider work of the church with arguably the most significant achievements being that, *'for the first time the laity have had a chance of discussing the role of the church and its work amongst them'.* Although *'in the past, we grew up believing that all decisions should be made by priests, we believe that this OD process is vital because we feel that people must own the church activities in their area'.*

Factors Constraining the Process
A number of factors were seen to constrain the process, including that:

- the consultants were seen to have too much other work, giving the impression that *'they do not have enough time for us'* and a fear of being left suspended;

- the OD process is also taking a lot of time and money leaving Sende, *'unable to devote so much time to our other development activities';*

- the donor lost their way a bit midway and tried to push the process too much, fixing it to artificial deadlines in the Hague (reminiscent of Robert Chambers comment that 'the harvesting cycles of donors and of Third World farmers are fundamentally different' (quoted in Morgan and Qualman 1996:14)). *'This was not compatible with the participative process we wanted and the size of the diocese and poor communications in the diocese and the fact that we were involved in a lot of other pastoral work'.*

- it was also seen that the *'OD process should not be done isolated from donor'* and would have benefited from understanding better their constraints. As one respondent said, *'if the donor wants openness from us they must be prepared to share their problems'.*

Factors Promoting the Process

A number of factors were identified which encouraged the effectiveness of this intervention, including:

- some leadership commitment. While some said that *'all along the bishop was championing the process'*, others felt that this was not the case originally, but it was the process itself that brought this commitment.

- The involvement of the whole organisation. The priests remain vital for implementation of any change programme so if they are uninvolved very little will change in practice.

- The process had to identify and manage the 'power-points' by having a political perspective and ensure that the internal OD group had enough power/ability and commitment to manage the change process. Conscious efforts were also made to build the capacity of this planning team through other inputs such as training.

- The Diocese of Sende put a lot of their own investment into the process, although not primarily in financial terms. Instead they put in massive time and *'extra effort and frustration'* on our part *'which proved to have a high cost on our children'.*

- The skills and attitudes of the consultants were lauded stating, *'the way they are performing is so beautiful'.* These consultants were seen to be much better than others, and *'we were surprised by their approach as they made us think for ourselves'*. As well as having the experience and the skills, they understood the organisation and the local context, *'they speak the language of the people, not just the development office'*

- The ongoing support of the donor. *'The idea originated from the donor, but then was taken up by the diocese'* but *'we wouldn't even have started without the assistance of the donor'*. The donor showed continued concern in the outputs and was prepared to see the process through.

RESTORING TRUST IN TRIPLE TRUST

A CDRA Intervention written up by *Rick James*

Introduction

In 1988, four South Africans came together with the idea of training unemployed people – who had little chance of getting a job – to start their own small businesses. Triple Trust Organisation (TTO) was formed and was quickly successful. Their activities soon attracted the attention of international donors and corporate sponsors and TTO was able to diversify and extend the range of services it could offer. In only five years, TTO grew from a small group of four to a large decentralised organisation employing 60–70 staff in 20 training centres throughout the Cape Town area.

This very success, however, nearly led to the downfall of TTO. While it brought solutions to others, TTO was not paying attention to its own organisational needs. The structure was no longer appropriate for the size of the organisation (with 17 departments all of which reported to two members of the senior management team); the founders (or pioneers) of the organisation had had to become managers; *'passion had given way to calls for form, policy and structure'* and there was considerable internal unrest with, *'staff disillusioned and even the threat of strike action'*.

As well as being symptomatic of rapid organisational growth, some of these problems were influenced by the massive changes in the external environment in South Africa during 1993/4 where everything was changing from white to black. The fight against apartheid had unified individuals and organisations, but when that enemy disappeared after the 1994 elections, people and organisations had to redefine their roles. NGOs were suddenly confronted by their own diversity. They had to deal with their own groups of blacks, whites, coloureds, working class, upper class, management and workers. The diversity had been there all along, but because the common focus was lost, conflict arose in the new era. Some of the pressures Triple Trust was facing were simply a microcosm of what was happening in the whole country.

Own Doctor

As a result TTO *'spent the year of 1994 trying to be our own doctor'*. There were many internal meetings and transitional committees with staff representative bodies and board member associations. Task groups on communication, terms of employment, structural change and cultural diversity were formed. Workshops were held on issues such as 'Unlearning Racism'.

While all this internal activity did give staff forums in which to express their views and showed that management was concerned and interested in their opinions, *'we weren't able to fix the problems'*.

By treating symptoms rather than causes, and the rational not the emotional, TTO experienced a year of gruelling accusation and counter accusation. The organisation was paralysed and limped along with programmes and concluded, *'we weren't getting anywhere on our own as it is very hard to diagnose issues of heart, values, culture yourself'* especially when loss of trust had become an issue and polarised staff and management.

In an act of desperation TTO sought help from CDRA (a very well respected South African organisation which provides OD consultancy support to the NGO sector).

The Intervention Process

CDRA developed an OD process which looked at four basic steps:

- examination and redefinition of the organisation's mission;
- examination and redefinition of their values;
- examination and redefinition of the organisation's structure;
- examination and rebuilding of perceptions, feelings and relationships.

They did this largely by means of an organisational survey, draft report and residential workshop.

CDRA Organisational Survey

In November 1994, two CDRA consultants (one white, one black) interviewed most of TTO staff to elicit their views, concerns and priorities. They found an organisation on the brink of collapse. Leadership and management, as roles and as concepts, were confused and contested. The staff felt they wanted a share in the ownership of the organisation and had been excluded so far. Trust had broken down and conflict and tension pervaded the whole organisation.

Report

From the interviews, the CDRA consultants produced a draft report and presented it to the staff and management at the end of December. Importantly, this report was a verbatim summary of what was said, a mirror without any consultant interpretation at that stage. The views of staff reflected in the report were seen by management as *'very damning': 'when we got CDRA's report we were confronted by stark reality. The report basically said our organisation was very sick, that it was run by three people who didn't listen to anyone else'*.

Another of the leadership team said the report was *'the stuff of suicides. So unbelievably awful. It was a big risk and we had to have lots of counselling to talk us out of resigning'*. The consultants in fact spent some time preparing the leadership team to receive the report (even taking them out to lunch!) and convincing them of their need to confront and deal with the issues rather than run away and resign.

Change Workshop

In order to deal with the issues raised in the report a five-day residential retreat for 40 staff members was arranged for December 1995. This was much more than a mere feedback meeting, but a strategic intervention for organisational change. Individual interviews, small group discussions and full group 'therapy sessions' were used to work through both rational and emotional issues. Issues raised in the report were written up as 'organisational norms' to provide insight into TTO culture. This statement of implicit norms, many of which were undesirable, provided the basis for a discussion of a set of values by which the organisation should operate, concluding by committing to paper a vision and values statement. It proved to be a 'very tough week'.

The retreat was seen by all as pivotal: *'we worked on the breaking down and building up of relationships. People cried; it was heart-wrenching for all of us. At one point we didn't think we were going to make it. But we did learn we had to improve relationships before we could restructure the organisation'*.

Resistance, anger, denial, attempted bargaining gave way to listening and trying to understand each other, relinquishing prejudice and preconceived perception. One of the founders concluded, *'at some point during the workshop, I had an ah-ha moment. I realised people were not saying that I was not doing a good job, but only that they wanted to share in helping us fulfil that vision'*.

Principles to guide the restructuring were developed as followed:

- information should be more freely available;
- decisions should be taken at a range of different levels;
- fewer departments with fewer lines to a central person;
- leadership should be wider and more focused.

CDRA then worked jointly with TTO to develop a structure which fulfilled these conditions.

This workshop was followed up immediately by two days back in the office. One day was for staff who could not be present at the workshop, and although the ground was covered, there was not the same group dynamics. Those who had not participated in the workshop said that they *'always felt a little robbed'*. The next day was spent discussing 'where do we go from here?'.

CDRA's work with TTO took about seven weeks spread over a nine-month period.

Preliminary Assessment of the Impact

The CDRA work clearly had a considerable impact on TTO, especially if it is compared with the 'control group' of TTO trying to solve its own problems without consultancy support. The senior management in particular attribute the CDRA work as ensuring the very survival of the organisation; *'that intervention rescued the organisation from complete disaster. It would have closed'*. Others said, *'the clarity of issues set us back on track'*... *'It was a real turning point'*.

At the very heart of OD consultancy is facilitating the NGO to take charge of its own development. The intervention indicated that this had been achieved to a certain extent as a *'structure was put in place where we can solve our own problems, before there were no systems or structures to catch these'*. The chair of the board has taken on the OD role – a monthly *'tapping of the wheel'*. When a new issue arose for example, senior management at TTO felt that *'if this current issue had happened before it would have been really serious, but now we can address it ourselves'*.

Certainly there are a number of organisational indicators to demonstrate that change has taken place to some degree:

Values: A values statement was developed which explained the kind of culture within which staff wanted to work.

Mission: The mission statement became more fully owned and understood by all staff.

Leadership: A broader and more mixed and representative leadership team was developed which resulted in *'the practice of leadership and management being no longer scorned but respected and is being practised in a coherent and organised fashion'*.

Strategy: Strategic planning processes were introduced.

Systems: HRD, strategic planning, monitoring and evaluation, teamwork and interdepartmental cooperation systems have all been initiated to some degree.

Relationships: Staff and management relationships improved considerably with *'a lot of barriers broken down'*.

Motivation: In order for staff to be motivated they need to have an understanding of the logic of the organisation. TTO was suffering from staff not having a sense of ownership of the organisation but *'that happened in that week'*... *'field workers now feel part of the organisation'*.

Impact on Beneficiaries: If an organisation is suffering from severe organisational problems then this will certainly be a significant constraint on their effectiveness as *'organisational problems affect the client very negatively'*. The TTO case showed that addressing these organisational ills will have a very real impact on beneficiaries: *'we were paralysed for one year before the intervention and our programmes were suffering'* ... *'Triple Trust field workers now have a place to be heard and are more empowered to do their own jobs'*.

Genuine transformation at a deep level is not easy, however, and there is the tendency to slip back into old patterns of behaviour. Some middle management staff in Triple Trust were more restrained in their assessment of the impact of the CDRA work feeling that the early momentum for change has been lost – *'the assumption was that we could continue on our own, but structures were not put in place, people were left untrained. When they left things fell back. The self-momentum carried things on for a while, but it soon waned'*.

They further point out that OD is not an event, but a process which needs to be continued within the organisation. *'CDRA was one event in the process and we see the workshop as a key part of our history'*. They believe that although TTO had the potential capacity to take on the change process itself it was not given enough priority and people were not *'empowered to take it on themselves'*. In fact some of the very changes, such as bringing more blacks into the leadership (who had not been part of the OD process), undermined its continuance.

Factors Constraining the Process

This case and the different perceptions about its effectiveness clearly highlight issues around follow-through. The consultant himself said, *'continuity in some form is key. One of the main problems with OD consultancy is the lack of follow-up; organisations feel they have moved beyond it'*. The consultant felt that insufficient follow-up had been given but that he had to wait to be asked back.

TTO were more equivocal, on the one hand saying, *'we have heard nothing since they left. The consultant felt we had the structure in place to support changes. But the new leadership was not part of that process and perhaps they could give us more follow-up'* and on the other noting that *'the temptation is to go back to the consultant all the time. We need to take ownership ourselves, and consultants need to hold back'*.

Even if the consultants themselves did not follow through, there was a feeling amongst some staff that the OD interventions were strengthened by greater staff development in these areas.

Factors Promoting the Process

External Consultants: The advantages of using external consultants was highlighted by many respondents stating that, *'we could not have gone through such a deep and painful process on our own. We needed an outsider'*.

Ownership: The most commonly mentioned success factor was that the NGO itself owned the change process and was prepared to invest in it, *'even if our funder had refused to support it we would have paid for it ourselves'*. The ownership of the change process is closely related to how keenly the NGO perceives the crisis. TTO were in the position of saying, *'we were at the wall. We had no choice'*.

Leadership: With the success of OD being closely related to the leadership's ability to shift, those who felt that Triple Trust had changed considerably attributed this partly to *'the willingness to face head on tough choices and be flexible'*.

Consultant: TTO took considerable time to find the right consultants sympathetic to TTO's beliefs, objectives and values. CDRA provided a very experienced, mixed black/white team. The style and skills of the consultants were crucial as they had to be able to lead TTO through very sensitive and at times conflictive processes. The main consultant was described as *'very skilled at trying to work through both the rational and the emotional'*.

Maturity of NGO: The maturity of the NGO was also seen to be a contributory factor in determining the success of OD. TTO said about their willingness to be open to change that *'we are capable people, and self-assured. We know we are doing good work we have nothing to hide we are not defensive'*.

Role of Donor: TTO lauded its donor in supporting this OD process saying that, *'we had a wonderful funder who two years before had asked us for a list of capacity-building projects and had funded 7 out of our list of 11'*. This donor, however, was not even a Northern NGO but a bilateral donor – the ODA (now DFID)! Such enlightened behaviour on the part of bilateral donors represents a very real challenge for Northern NGOs. The role of donor was strictly limited to the funding of the consultancy and was not involved in the OD process itself. The CDRA was contracted and reported exclusively to TTO.

TUBA[1] – SUFFERING FROM SUCCESS?

Rick James

Introduction

The Umbrella Body for Aids (TUBA) was established in 1993 by a number of different local and international development agencies in Malawi. They were all increasingly concerned at the rising prevalence of Aids in Malawi and hoped to share experience and learning. TUBA was to facilitate the coordination and cooperation of NGOs, donors and government involved in Aids-related projects.

TUBA quickly secured funding and established a good reputation through its coherent and articulate leadership; its high calibre staff; and regular and useful national coordination meetings and newsletters. Within a short period of time TUBA was credible and trusted with its major donor saying, *'it's one NGO we are proud of'*.

By 1996, TUBA had grown to 12 staff members and was diversifying its activities into a number of related roles. As well as working on coordination, information and networking activities amongst NGOs, international donors and government, TUBA was also training communities in Aids awareness education; training NGOs and government extension staff in community care and counselling methods and medical aspects to Aids prevention and care; undertaking research and advisory support in gender-related aspects of development; starting an Aids resource centre; undertaking district-level coordination of NGOs involved in Aids care; as well as channelling funds to NGOs as part of a World Bank programme of Aids management. TUBA had already been involved in policy level discussions on Malawi's Aids prevention and care policy and was also contemplating taking a more active advocacy role towards government as well as being asked by a number of international bodies to be a regional focal point.

Potential Crisis?

This growth and diversification soon began to cause a number of internal pressures. TUBA leadership and staff were feeling increasingly overworked and unable to complete all their tasks adequately. There was a concern that performance and reputation would soon suffer. Staff morale was falling and programmes were operating in an isolated fashion.

It was clear to the leadership, as well as to the staff, that TUBA was being

---

[1] Fictitious name and programme focus.

dangerously overstretched and that they needed to better define their role in the future and develop a more focused strategy. This desire coincided with the concerns of a prospective donor; and as part of the first year's funding (and the indication that funding would be for at least three to five years) a grant was included for TUBA to undertake a strategic directions exercise.

The Intervention Process

A few months earlier TUBA had met and quickly built up a level of understanding and trust with a British OD consultant doing a short-term contract in Malawi. The donor had considerable contact with and was favourably disposed to the NGO with whom this consultant worked and so TUBA approached the consultant to undertake this work.

Much of the planning had to be done by fax; during which time:

- it was arranged that TUBA would contract the consultant, not the donor, and that a Malawian consultant would be contracted to work alongside the expatriate;
- the different roles and responsibilities of TUBA and the consultants were agreed;
- TUBA's ownership of the need for the intervention was identified;
- the process was designed for undertaking the work;
- the outputs of the work were clearly defined – TUBA maintained responsibility for writing up any action points into a revised strategic plan and a capacity-building plan;
- a questionnaire for staff and another for partner NGOs was designed and sent.

The initial process was agreed at two weeks with a follow-up visit from the consultants after six months. While the limitations of such a discrete exercise were understood, it was decided that a limited initial process would not preclude further involvement later should more ongoing support prove necessary.

On arrival, the consultants spent a day with the director of TUBA discovering the background to the consultancy and what was expected from the intervention. The key stakeholders in TUBA had previously been identified and individual meetings had been arranged with all TUBA staff, most of TUBA board members, a sample of Malawian NGOs involved with TUBA, TUBA international donors and contractors (such as the World Bank) and other stakeholders such as the national umbrella body for NGOs and the government ministry of health.

The two consultants spent seven days gathering data on TUBA from:

- the semi-structured interviews;
- the questionnaire responses from TUBA staff and member NGOs;
- a review of past TUBA plans, reports and evaluations.

The data was analysed and structured by the consultants and discussed with 15 members of TUBA staff and board during the four-day workshop which followed the interviews.

Strategic Directions Workshop

The aim of the workshop was to get the TUBA staff and board to diagnose for themselves where they thought TUBA was at the moment. This included both an internal diagnosis and an analysis of the current and future threats and opportunities in the external environment. Their analysis was complemented and developed by the findings from the consultants' previous data-gathering process. The workshop then facilitated participants to determine which of TUBA's clients were they really there to serve and what did this client group want from TUBA. This prioritising process enabled TUBA to decide what core role it wanted to play. On the basis of this choice the mission statement was reworked and gender-related objectives were included.

The workshop then introduced a role-play visioning exercise for board and staff to dream of where they wished TUBA to be in four years time and the common themes were highlighted. The discrepancy between where TUBA was today and where it wanted to be was then analysed by participants, and the strategic issues which needed to be dealt with in order to get there were identified. In working groups, the external/programming strategic options were discussed and decided upon and the internal issues (such as the lack of a 'team-working' culture, limited gender awareness, delayed decision-making, and inappropriate systems for internal controls and staff recruitment and development) were also analysed and solutions proposed. The outputs of these working groups were synthesised during plenary feedback. The consultants refused to write up this information. Rather they encouraged the formation of two small voluntary teams to take responsibility for writing up the feedback into a strategic plan and an organisational development plan by a certain date after the workshop. The closure of the workshop involved some 'reality testing' by applying the strategic decisions that had been made to actual and contentious programmes. This testing revealed a coherence amongst the staff and the board of the fairly momentous implications of the decisions they had made – such as withdrawing from the funding role which the World Bank was encouraging them to take on.

Factors Promoting the Process

The **leadership** was extremely committed to the process, both the chair of the board and chief executive were leading the process.

TUBA was a **young and flexible** organisation in an early stage of its development which meant it had not picked up too much bureaucratic baggage and vested interests' leaving it open to change.

The process was also helped by TUBA being small enough for the entire organisation to be **actively** involved in the process.

There was sufficient pain being experienced in terms of feeling over-stretched and declining morale to preclude the maintenance of the status quo. Unless key people in the organisation **feel the need for change** (pain) none is likely to occur.

There was **general agreement amongst all stakeholders** (staff, board, partner NGOs, donors, contractors) on the issues which TUBA needed to address. There was a critical mass of support for change and no great conflict in direction.

The donor was flexible enough to let TUBA direct and contract the consultancy process. Their long-term view of a funding relationship with TUBA enabled TUBA to lengthen its strategic perspective and not just go for quick bucks.

TUBA themselves invested a lot in the process. The chief executive made it clear to staff that this was the priority for their time and TUBA themselves covered the not inconsiderable workshop costs

While the workshop ended on a high note, it was recognised that the real problems would arise in implementing the decisions.

Disaster Strikes!

Within one month of the workshop, the director of TUBA was found to have been defrauding TUBA of large amounts of money over the past six months. He was immediately sacked. Despite the fact that many of the Malawian staff suspected this to have been the case, the local and international consultant both missed diagnosing this area of weakness for a number of reasons:

- the accountant who had all the information was recovering from a motorbike accident during the whole consultancy (and staff were looking to him to expose the fraud)!;
- the other staff who knew of the fraud felt implicated because they had done nothing to date, fearing for their jobs;
- Malawian cultural norms do not promote confrontation and exposure of others and have a great respect for those in authority (one Chichewa proverb encapsulates this sentiment – wamkulu sawuzidwa – 'he is old, therefore he is right');
- failure on the consultants' behalf to probe the 'mud' of the organisation

more thoroughly;
- by focusing on strategy, the intervention missed some of the underlying values of honesty and integrity.

This demonstrates the need for OD consultancies to look at some of the harder financial issues in some detail; to be aware of the resistance of many people to publicly expose their leaders; and to probe further when off-hand comments are dropped. Having said that, if the consultancy had managed to expose the fraud issue this would have undoubtedly derailed the strategic planning process which would have left TUBA without a direction and without a director (as opposed to just without a director!).

Preliminary Assessment of the Impact

While the strategic plan was written up by the staff after the workshop and approved by the board, TUBA has continued to face difficulties. The decision to withdraw from channelling World Bank funds angered the Bank and so, with the departure of the director, the Bank was soon able to say publicly that it was this mismanagement of funds which had led the World Bank to pull out of TUBA, not vice versa. Within a month of the loss of the director, the Chair of the Board and two foreign volunteers have also left the country (as their contracts had ended) aggravating the leadership vacuum. This has severely inhibited the implementation of the change process, both strategically and in terms of addressing the identified capacity-building needs.

Almost 12 months after the departure of the director, the leadership vacuum still has not been filled – one director who was appointed by the board was clearly unsuited and his contract was terminated after just one month. The foreign consultant (now resident in Malawi) has continued with limited involvement with TUBA in an informal counselling role with some of the remaining staff. Donors too were increasingly worried about the situation and were being presented with proposals for funding which were patently unrealistic. Just as it looked as though they would withdraw support and TUBA would collapse, a final opportunity was given to TUBA to revise their proposal. The remaining staff led this process themselves and with donor support asked the consultant to help facilitate a one-day programme planning day to help them develop some of their strategic priorities into a fundable proposal. The proposal which the staff developed was greeted extremely enthusiastically by donors – 'it has improved 200%'.

This process, for all its limitations of implementation, did result in a small NGO gaining sufficient self-identity to be able to say no to the World Bank and perhaps more importantly did succeed in broadening the 'ownership' of the organisation amongst the staff. Prior to the workshop much of the understanding of the rationale and direction of TUBA lay entirely in the director's head. If this understanding had not been transferred to the rest of the staff, it is unlikely that TUBA would have been able to survive the succeeding 11 months of leadership chaos. It also reinforces the extent to which responsibility for actually bringing about organisational change lies not with the consultants, but with the NGO itself.

IN THE WAKE OF CONFLICT

The Eritrean War Disabled Fighters' Association (EWDFA)

Organisational Self-Definition and Planning Process

Daudi Waithaka

Introduction

The Eritrean War Disabled Fighters' Association (EWDFA) was founded as an 'NGO' with the encouragement and support of the Government of Eritrea. Unlike many other newly independent countries where existing elites take over, the ex-soldiers in Eritrea formed a major part of the new government. This government realised it had an enormous debt to the disabled fighters and had a duty to support their resettlement and rehabilitation. It also soon realised that it could not support them from the national budget for ever and that an organisation owned, controlled and run by the disabled themselves would have the best potential to address their long-term needs for medical care and economic resources.

In 1992 and 1993, the government gave EWDFA considerable grants as well as contracts for beer distribution throughout the country to help the NGO get off the ground. A draft constitution was approved by a founding Congress, members recruited, offices established, core staff hired and programmes started. These programme initiatives, however, did not prove successful as the ex-fighters had very little experience of civilian business and management. The programme stagnation soon resulted in internal quarrels over direction and increasing tension between the civilian and military elements and the disabled and non-disabled members. While the desire to contribute was there and the funding was also there, these did not translate into effective programmes.

The EWDFA approached Norwegian Church Aid (NCA) (as Norwegian organisations had always been very close to the struggle in Eritrea) to see how their organisation could be made more effective. Through discussions NCA suggested that a Kenyan consultancy firm, Matrix, be approached to help facilitate two parallel processes – a five-day workshop with one group to look at vision and mission, as well as a three-day workshop with another group to look at constitutional issues.

On reviewing the literature on the organisation and its history, the Kenyan consultant felt that the approach suggested was too superficial to deal with the significant problems of identity in an organisation of 18,000 members and yet with little idea of who it was, what it wanted to be, how to resolve inherent con-flicts internally as well as how it should relate to others externally. It was thought that a one-off vision workshop might create a vision statement, but would probably not create a shared vision. A longer-term intervention was sug-gested which would also keep the entire group of 20 executive committee mem-bers and senior staff together. These suggestions were agreed to both by EWDFA and by NCA.

The Intervention Process

A staggered series of workshops took place with the aims of:

- training the participants in the art of analytical planning;
- analysing the current situation in the country and of the members with a view to mapping out the organisation's place in the development of both;
- highlighting issues and areas of weakness in the organisation to collectively prescribe potential solutions and actions;
- concurrently and practically applying those skills gained to actually produce a 1997 Annual Plan and Five Year Plan.

Workshop I: Vision and Mission (ten days) early 1996

A visioning process was used so that the participants defined:

- what the fighters ought to be like;
- how to get to that desired future;
- what the organisation should be like to facilitate that process.

In between the workshops participants were required to do a lot of 'homework' identifying what sorts of activity each of the categories of the disabled could do and what they needed to be able to do these. Mini-workshops throughout the country were held which helped members feel greater ownership of the process. These wider consultations were written up with the help of NCA-supplied sec-retarial and translation services.

Workshop II: Strategies and Main Activities (seven days)

In this workshop the main approaches and activities were outlined bringing together the findings of the wider consultations.

Back in the communities after the workshop, participants continued the process of consultation by working out how these activities might be imple-mented. For example, activities such as providing institutional care for the severely disabled had to deal with questions of implementation including who will supply the medicines and how will it be paid for in the long term.

Workshop III: Detailed 1997 Annual Plan and Sketch of Five Year Plan (14 days) late 1996

The actual plans for 1997 and 1998 were detailed with the workshop participants brainstorming the contents of the planning document and then authorising one person to write it up. A very detailed operational plan and budget was arrived at.

These plans were then translated and taken to regional workshops for discussion and further refinement.

Towards the end of 1997 a review is planned to find out what has gone right and what has gone wrong and what can be learnt. So far about ten weeks consultancy time has been taken, spread out over the course of the year.

Preliminary Assessment of the Impact

There is evidence of positive impact in a number of areas:

- Vision and mission statements were produced – a 'first' for an Eritrean organisation.
- Overall strategies were produced, including a 5 year plan with an indicative budget.
- A detailed annual plan with budgets was produced.
- Participant skills were enhanced as evidenced by their evaluations.
- Cultural shift – despite the military culture which pervaded at the start, decision-making has become more consultative and decentralised with regular meetings formalised.
- Conflict resolution – civilians and combatant colleagues are now happier working together.

Factors Constraining the Process

The main languages of the participants were Arabic and Tigrigna. The Kenyan consultant had to communicate in English and so there was a need for good translation and interpretation. Communication became much more difficult.

The consultant was an outsider and a stranger to an organisation which had a very strong common history of struggle and yet were now disabled. There was much resistance to an able-bodied outsider who had not fought in the war. This meant that the consultant had to be very open about himself and his own history to gain acceptance, proving that he did understand their context and developing sufficient rapport with the fighters to reach even a point of sharing jokes about their disabilities.

Factors Promoting the Process

The climate in the country was very conducive to the organisation. The disabled fighters were revered throughout society for their sacrifice in the struggle. The government was very supportive giving them comfortable funding and removing a big burden of having to respond to donor demands.

The organisation was truly motivated and committed to change. They recognised they had reached a point of stagnation and if they did not help themselves who would do it for them.

The combatants had an extremely strong team spirit. They were used to working together. They had been sharing their beliefs, pains and dreams for many years.

The top leadership gave their full commitment to the entire process as all members of the Executive Committee and senior staff participated fully.

The consultant spent considerable time in learning the context and history of the organisation and its struggle as well as the Eritrean culture. The consultant also prepared case histories of other struggles in Africa to apply back to their situation.

The donor funded the consultancy and provided all the necessary transport, translation services, secretarial services as well as stationery resources. They recognised the need for an ongoing process in the wider organisation, rather than just one-off workshops. They held back from full participation in the early workshops as they would have been tempted to try to move the process too quickly. At subsequent workshops they were able to be a bit more involved as EWDFA was beginning to establish a clearer self-identity. The donor also separated the OD process from a funding decision. The first stage of OD is building confidence – this cannot be done within the context of a donor decision on funding as *'NGOs have to find their feet first and feel they can argue with a donor on an equal basis and that disagreement on certain issues is OK'*.

INTEGRATING OD

Namibian Rural Development NGO (NRDN)[2]

Lynette Maart (CDRA)

Introduction

The NRDN had been established in 1987 as a channel for development aid money from the European Economic Community (EEC) to Victims of Apartheid. It aimed to fund local NGOs and CBOs involved in resistance work. In 1990 South Africa finally withdrew from their occupation of Namibia in the face of increased international pressure and the looming possibility of military defeat. The South West African People's Organisation (SWAPO) won a landslide victory in the first democratic election in 1990. It soon became clear, however, that it was unable to deliver on its election promises of alleviating poverty due to a number of factors including very limited human and financial resources.

After independence the NRDN redefined itself as a national service organisation and changed its focus to facilitate the development of NGOs and CBOs in the areas of education, health, agriculture, income generation, organisation development, gender research, as well as lobbying, networking and advocacy. By 1993 the NRDN employed 22 staff members, all of whom were Namibian locals. The organisation prides itself in that it has no European or white person on its staff. The NRDN is based in Windhoek, with field offices in the South and North of Namibia.

The Aim of the Intervention

In December 1992 the CDRA received a letter from a Dutch-based funding agency requesting the CDRA to assist the NRDN with a routine three-year evaluation process that would cover:

- an assessment of the impact of the organisation's work;
- internal organisational development, for example, leadership/management, structuring to support the focus, staff development and policies and procedures.

The donor was also concerned about funding, questioning whether they should

---

[2] Not the real name.

continue to invest in Namibia. The CDRA responded to the funder's request that it preferred dealing directly with the client rather than through a third party. The CDRA believes that development can only be nurtured where the freedom and integrity of the client, as well as the relationship between the consultant and the client, is sacrosanct. Therefore, the CDRA asked the NRDN to make a request for an evaluation process in its own name. It received such a request from the NRDN in February 1993.

The Intervention Process

Initially the CDRA thought that an evaluation and strategic planning process (three months in 1993) would be sufficient to boost the staff capacity. However, the intervention took three years and three phases:

1. entry and developing a strategic framework for the way forward;
2. developing the capacity of leadership and management;
3. developing the capacity of the field-work and programme staff.

Each phase was negotiated and contracted for separately. At times the needs emerged out of conversations with the organisation and at other times it was based on suggestions from the consultants as to what could be a potential next step. The NRDN then negotiated with its existing funders or sought new funders to support a particular part of the intervention.

Phase One: Entry, diagnosis and developing a strategic framework for the way forward.

Most of the negotiation for the first phase took place over the telephone and by letter. In the initial contract with the NRDN the CDRA agreed to:

- conduct an organisational survey which would enable the CDRA to gain an in-depth understanding of the functioning of the Namibian NGO. The survey would be focused on both the internal organisational environment (vision and mission, management of resources and functioning of the organisation) and the external context (i.e. communities that the NGO works with and the broader Namibian context influencing the dynamic within these communities);

- conduct an organisational workshop that would allow the NRDN to explore its issues and develop skills as well as adequate plans to resolve these issues and move into the future and complete the report of the process;

- undertake future work as the need arises.

This part of the contract was carried out by two CDRA consultants over a three-month period in 1993. Phases two and three are described in detail under the section titled: The Closure and Next Steps Taken.

The Implementation
The following methods were used:

1. Organisational survey

This process took three weeks. The time frame was influenced by distances. During this phase the CDRA interviewed NRDN clients and board members and identified role-players in the Namibian NGO community. The CDRA visited project sites and the respective offices to observe their functioning. It also carried out a review of relevant organisational literature. This enabled the CDRA to develop overviews of the history and work of the NRDN and the changing Namibian context; analysis of the work done with clients; and an assessment of the internal organisational functions focusing on identity, strategies, personnel, technical support and systems, structures and procedures and leadership and management.

The results of the organisational survey were written up in a draft report.

2. Organisational workshop

In a one-week residential workshop the CDRA assisted staff to work through the issues raised in the draft diagnostic and evaluation report and devised a strategic response for addressing these including overhauling the technical sub-system of the organisation.

3. Final report

The final report incorporated the changes and comments made by staff of the interim report during the first part of the workshop. The final report also contained the outcomes of the organisational workshop and future recommendations by the consultants.

The Closure and Next Steps Taken
This process ended (according to the first contract) after the organisational workshop. During the workshop, however, we were confronted with the reality of the leadership and management capacity of an organisation staffed primarily by Namibians. It was extremely difficult just to walk away. Over the next two and a half years, while not part of the initial plan, the following interventions

became appropriate and were conducted as the NRDN developed.

Phase Two: Developing the capacity of the management team (three-year project from 1994 to 1996).

The second phase comprised the following steps:

- a workshop in 1994 which targeted the newly appointed leadership of the NRDN to explore the tasks and functions of organisational leadership and management and self-management;
- three members of the management team attended the CDRA – Facilitating Organisation Development (FOD) Course in 1994 and another one in 1995;
- evaluation and strategic planning with the entire management team for one week in 1995 and another week in 1996 to tackle internal functioning and management difficulties.

Phase Three: Developing the capacity of the field-work staff (one year 1996).

This included accompanying the entire field team (15 staff) through the Fieldworkers' Formation Course (FFC) in 1996, a training and development programme designed to equip participants to better facilitate the building of capacity of clients.

Preliminary Assessment of the Impact

Clarity was gained in the identity, purpose and strategies of the NRDN and then refined even more in 1995 when the organisation defined itself as working in the area of poverty alleviation through attaining household food security and more specifically agriculture and income generation and capacity-building of local initiatives. The OD interventions resulted in very real changes in strategy with programmes actually being closed down – *'NRDN, a generalist organisation decided to concentrate on agriculture and income generation. They dropped pre-school education, health, resource centres and libraries'*. This did not remain a one-off event, as ongoing strategic planning processes were introduced.

There were very real changes in the style of leadership and organisational culture, with *'the pioneer culture which knew about everything and was responsive to all demands giving way to a more differentiated way of working where strategic choices were made'*.

A radical restructuring of the organisation resulting in three decentralised offices and a national office with the role of providing organisational and financial support while *'regional managers were given a role in determining the organisational direction'*. The restructuring process took the organisation approximately one and a half years to complete. It had to secure financial resources and to search from within its ranks and outside for potentially suitable leadership candidates and then train them.

Development of leadership and management capacity took place. Without this, the initial intervention would not have been sustained. The CDRA firmly believes that organisational development is intertwined with the capacity of leadership and management collectively and as individuals. An indication of this is that the pioneer leader has indicated that she is willing to move on to greener pastures, as some leadership and management capacity has been developed. She would not have been able to risk this during 1993. There was also the development of staff skills at field level which led to an *'increased level of analysis and depth of questions at field-worker level. They became able to critique and change their own practice'.*

Most importantly, the organisation in the short term dealt with the immediate crisis but also created the institutional framework upon which further capacity could be built. Even though the process has been slow and at times painstaking it has enabled the staff of the NRDN to improve their understanding of their roles within the organisation and of the organisational functioning overall, thus putting the NRDN in a better position to make conscious and informed choices for the organisation's future development.

Key Learnings

When confronted with the outcome of the initial diagnostic report the organisational leadership (the director – a coloured female and the deputy director – black male) took the criticism as a personal attack on their integrity. Their initial reaction was panic, withdrawal and paralysis. A lot of counselling work was done on the side with the director and she concluded, *'this was my moment of consciousness. I needed to be shocked to make the shift'.*

In order to encourage this change the consultants had to use different consulting styles, such as both the confrontational and the nurturing style. The consultants felt that *'you need both roles, especially in organisations of women where confrontation is very difficult for them to deal with'.*

It is clear from this case that the context is important in affecting the nature of OD. By consciously choosing to employ only black staff (with a limited educational background) it *'means that the OD process will take longer and be more expensive. It is making up for years of poor education which means you cannot take the knowledge base for granted. Also Namibia has a much smaller pool to draw on than South Africa which makes the pace slower'.*

While the CDRA intervention was meant to scale down the activities of the NGO and provide capacity-building (allowing the donor to exit), CDRA was clear at the outset to the donor *'if you want to exit then say so, but do not use an evaluation to do so'*. The donor is still there to this day.

During the intervention the staff of the NRDN needed time in between interventions to digest what happened, to distil learnings and to take forward in implementation what was useful for them. This required considerable patience of the consultant and the ability to hold back. This holding back at times, and not giving up, is vital to the success of an intervention of this nature, particularly with local African initiatives which tend to have organisational capacity constraints. Organisation development is not a one-night stand based only on the needs and requirement of funders. It is a long-term relationship that is based on mutual understanding and respect.

Factors Promoting the Process

NRDN maintained ownership of the intervention. At the start CDRA insisted that the request for the support come from NRDN and that the contracting be done directly by them rather than by the Dutch donor. The feedback workshop process in Phase one continued this ownership of the issues. CDRA did not just extract information to write a report, but they used this to design the workshop for NRDN to work through the strategic issues and responses. The consultants also showed the importance of holding back from becoming too directive and ensuring that control remained with the NRDN.

The intervention recognised the long-term nature of organisational change and did not expect that a one-off workshop would solve all NRDN's problems. Extensive follow-up was given.

This follow-up used a mixture of other capacity-building methodologies such as training, highlighting the benefit of a multi-pronged approach to organisational change.

The diagnostic process enabled the consultants to gain an in-depth understanding of the key issues which NRDN needed to address and undoubtedly helped them facilitate the workshop appropriately and manage the initial adverse reactions of the leadership.

The intervention shows the importance of ensuring that the leadership is fully involved in the process, not just consenting to it. If the director had not been given such one-to-one counselling support, she may well have derailed the entire process.

A THERAPIST'S THERAPY

An Organisational Review of Olive (OD&T)

David Harding

Introduction

This case study is of a review process carried out over three weeks in November and December of 1996 with a South African intermediary level NGO, Olive (OD&T), that specialises in support to other NGOs – particularly through organisational assessment and development work, strategic management and training in development management and organisational issues.

Olive is relatively young – founded in 1993. It has grown from a small core of staff supporting one key professional (the founder, now director) to an organisation with a professional 'delivery' team of six staff in its core area of work; a small but internationally valued publications service with two staff; some 'spin-off' projects; and an administrative/support team of around six staff.

The organisation has a very good reputation with both clients and donors. It is sought after and widely recognised as both effective in its work and friendly and supportive in its engagement.

For the previous two years Olive had held an annual review of its work facilitated and led by an external overseas consultant. Olive sought OD consultancy support even in their first year without facing any particular crisis, simply on the grounds that *'a therapist needs therapy'*. They were looking for outside support to be *'another pair of eyes, bringing a new perspective and constantly bringing us up to the mark'*. In 1996 the organisation wanted to repeat what it saw as a useful exercise but with a broader framework of reference.

The Aim of the Intervention

The ToR drawn up for the 1996 review were:

- to assess the role Olive has played and its possible future role over the next three years;
- to consider the views of funders, clients and collegial organisations to assess Olive's services in terms of relevance, quality and availability;
- to consider staff, the Board and user views to assess Olive's levels of competence, effectiveness and efficiency in conducting its work;
- to assess the extent to which the suggestions from the 1995 review have been taken up or not and reasons for this;
- to comment on Olive's sustainability strategies;

- to recommend any changes or shifts to improve Olive's positioning, its work and its impact.

For this exercise it was thought that the external consultant should be complemented by a local consultant with management experience in the NGO sector and a strong background in development. Given the increased size and complexity of the organisation and the broader scope of the review, a different perspective on Olive was sought. The facilitators had limited experience working together but knew enough of each other's work and approaches to key issues to feel that they would work well together.

The Intervention Process

The review team interviewed over 40 people in three weeks – Olive staff and associates, board members and a range of clients and donors. The interviews generally lasted between one and two hours, and the overwhelming majority were conducted face to face. The team also had access to any Olive documentation, internal and published, that they needed. Towards the end of the review process the team worked through some of their provisional findings and thoughts with the director as a 'checking' process. The review team then met with all Olive staff over one day to report on the key issues that they had been alerted to, and their own judgements on these. A final report, summarising the day's discussions was then drawn up.

In conducting the review in this way the review team and Olive were quite consciously following a particular approach for attempting to understand organisational effectiveness and surfacing key issues. This could be summarised as:

- a lightly structured approach moving between semi-structured interviews and documentary research and with a continuous and intensive dialogue between the review team members to identify issues arising;
- an iterative approach which re-focused interviews and reading as issues surfaced (e.g. including, where possible, returning to some interviewees to re-visit themes which had later acquired more importance);
- using initial assumptions about Olive and its issues as a starting-point;
- an open interview process which began with the interviewees own experience of Olive and sought to explore with them their sense of key issues.

There are several reasons for the consultants favouring this open exploratory approach:

- As in many organisational review processes, the team had no basis for anticipating what would be the eventual underlying key issues (often different to some of the initial 'presenting' issues). There was no basis for pre-structuring interviews or other work to focus in on certain themes or areas.

- The review team wanted to build as 'whole' a picture of Olive as possible, from a multitude of perspectives before starting to attempt to identify key areas. The team was not over-worried therefore about being submerged in information, but more concerned not to predetermine or prematurely close down on discussion.
- The team felt from its experience that imposing a heavy structure on interviews often cuts across and disrupts the energy and thoughts interviewees bring to a review discussion.
- The review team's experience was that critical issues often emerge first as patterns across different interviews and readings, but often not as central themes in any one interview. The team needs to be constantly reviewing the 'picture' that is building, picking up possible patterns and then re-focusing on them to develop and check.

Working the Review Process

The review work began on 12 November with consultants working separately in different areas of the country, talking to Olive client NGOs and funders. The review team came together in Durban on 25 November and then worked jointly for the next ten days on interviews and background reading with Durban-based clients, other NGOs working with Olive, staff and board members.

The interviews with client and donor organisations quickly confirmed an overall positive view of Olive's work and effectiveness. Getting to grips with key issues or concerns that might nevertheless have been present in the encounters(s) with Olive proved more difficult. Few organisations had a clearly thought out position on the quality of Olive's work and any misgivings or issues which may have arisen. Issues emerged as odd thoughts, as asides, as a tentative suggestion or were sometimes implicit.

The interviews with staff were generally more dynamic with issues stated more clearly – in itself perhaps a positive sign of Olive's openness as an organisation. What became clear quite quickly was that there were some important, sensitive and quite painful issues underneath the 'light and funky' impression of Olive and its office at work. There also seemed to be some very basic issues of approach and practice around both development management and organisational areas of work.

A significant gap in the interview process was with the Olive board. In the end, despite attempts to reschedule appointments, the review team met only one member of the board apart from the Chair. This did reflect deeper problems with the composition and commitment of the Board which were brought up in the review report. It also, however, reflected the position of a 'hands-off' board which saw Olive as working very well without its undue interference.

Despite the difficulties in the interviews with clients and funders the review team very quickly began to build up a very rich picture of Olive and its work. Potential issues also emerged quite quickly in three main areas:

• fundamental issues of approach, practice and effectiveness in Olive's work on development management and organisational support;
• a number of key management issues – the role of the director, of the board, and in the area of financial management;
• some important and potentially conflictive issues around culture and internal organisational relations and structure.

The one area where almost all of the interviews failed to produce significant results was that of recommendations on Olive's future direction. At the time of the review development policy in South Africa was in a transitional period and the prospects for NGOs within overall policy seemed even more transitional and uncertain. Again too few of those interviewed seemed to have a good enough grasp of some of the macro-level issues facing the NGO sector to comment on possible future trends. The combination of these factors meant that the review team finally were left very much to contribute only their own thoughts in this area.

With all issues the review team sought to get a cross-check of positions – whether that came from other interviews, documents or further meetings with the person who initially raised it. In the end, however, much depended on the judgement of the two consultants in the review team; their own approach to, and understanding of, key areas of theory and practice; and a largely subjective set of evidence which the consultant's had to weigh and assess.

As a final check of their work the team met with the Director of Olive to discuss the provisional picture that the review work had built up. The team also discussed with the Director at this point the proposed structure and process for the 'report-back' day. It should be emphasised that in the discussion with the Director both sides were clear that the review team was *presenting* and *checking* its work, not, at this point, seeking confirmation or approval from the Director of the issues arising or the overall conclusions of the team.

Reporting Back on the Review

The intention of the review team was always to present a report to Olive at the end of the review work which would serve as a *basis for discussion* for Olive for the coming period. This had been the practice in previous reviews and had worked well. The review team believed it was not the role of external consultants to make detailed recommendations or set standards or goals for the organisation to respond to. The review report back should seek to outline issues and promote discussion around them. The review team was confident that Olive was an open and mature organisation able to take on board issues and work through them itself. Additionally as an OD support organisation it needed to be able to do this if it was to help other organisations follow the same analytical and strategic response path.

These good intentions were undermined by the lack of time scheduled for the reporting back process – only one day. The review exercise threw up a wealth of issues, many intertwined, and ranging from broad thematic concerns down to detailed issues and questions. The richness and complexity of the picture made any attempt at presentation in detail impossible in a one-day session. The reviewers decided therefore to attempt to isolate the most important issues and set these out succinctly in the form of a set of 'recommendations', with time and opportunity for discussion around the key issues, drawing in other issues where relevant.

The reporting-back process was further complicated by the fact that Olive had asked several representatives of key funders to be present during at least part of the report-back day. While contributing greatly to the 'transparency' of discussion with funders their presence was bound to put some limits on openness of discussion.

The consultants did not get the balance right in the report-back day. The size of the group and its heterogeneity meant that there was little good discussion of the issues raised. Staff were overwhelmed both by the issues themselves and the weight of information in even the limited presentation. Some of the argument from the review team was too heavyweight, conceptually and linguistically, for the administrative and support team staff who felt left behind and left out of any discussion that did ensue. The presence of funders did cut across the mood of the group and prevented a flow of open discussion. The funders struggled to get to grips with the review's breadth and some of the issues and their own questions revealed different concerns perhaps from those of Olive staff.

Overall reaction to the report-back day was therefore mixed. Some staff saw 'their' issues flagged up and were overall pleased with the review; others were less happy with the intensity of the analysis and the 'tough' tone; still others regretted the limited scope for discussion; many felt that the consultants had presented an overwhelming set of 'issues' without giving much help in indicating priorities or urgency of address (the review team tackled this concern in their written report).

The reaction to the *process* of the 'report back' cut across, at the time, the general reaction to the *content* of the review. Later reaction from Olive assessed the review as very useful in having raised some very key tough issues. Overall there was a recognition that all the issues raised were indeed valid, although there was continuing discussion about detail, importance and priority.

Preliminary Assessment of the Impact

Olive itself has said that the review provided it with a very useful framework for strategic discussion which it had to have and did have in subsequent months. The process was said to *'bring focus back to the organisation'* and forced Olive to slow down and take stock, *'reinforcing our reflective culture'*. In the original thinking on the review the idea of providing a critical frame of reference – to be discussed, hacked at, owned or disowned – was seen as one of the primary purposes of the review. In that sense the work, despite the important problems with reporting back, could be said to have achieved at least part of its purpose and to have helped Olive move forward at a critical transitional point for the organisation.

Part Three

Learning from OD Practice

Chapter 4

The ODC Processes

INTRODUCTION

The preparation for the research project involved asking Northern NGOs what key questions they had about the practice of ODC. This next section seeks to provides a response to some of those questions in the light of the case studies presented. Chapter 4 focuses on the OD process looking at the following questions:

- Why were the OD interventions requested?
- What were the main triggers?
- What were the key ODC entry points?
- What types of method were used?
- What were the OD processes used?
- How long did they last?
- What was the relationship between OD and other methods of capacity-building?
- Where were the consultants based?
- Should consultants work in teams or alone?

This chapter considers the processes used by the OD consultants to discern the extent of deviation from the ideal theory presented in Chapter 2.

THE ODC PROCESS IN PRACTICE

Why were the OD Interventions Requested?
<u>External Factors</u>
Adapting to Changes in the External Environment
The OD interventions described in the preceding case studies demonstrate how changes in the external environment forced NGOs to change and adapt. The

1990s have seen massive changes in the NGO sector as a whole as well as considerable changes in national NGO sectors, lending weight to the assertion that the 1990s really are 'turbulent times' for NGOs. The changes which have taken place in South Africa over the last five years have totally altered the NGO landscape. NGOs were traditionally set up to counter the impact of the apartheid system. When the ANC assumed power, NGOs had to rethink totally their relationship and attitude to government which often involved questioning their very identity and reason for existing. These external changes were certainly prime factors in bringing about the need for OD processes with TTO and the Fellowship of Churches. Similarly, the independence of Namibia forced NRDN to rethink its mission and strategy. In Eritrea, independence meant that the EWDFA was able to form with the help of the government. Likewise in Malawi, the replacement of autocratic rule three years ago not only permitted NGOs much greater freedom to establish, but also the resumption and prioritisation of international aid to Malawi has made funding for NGOs much easier to access, forcing new NGOs such as TUBA to quickly have to deal with problems of growth.

Funding changes in Europe over the last five years, with 'back' donor governments pushing international NGOs for much greater evidence of results, have had a knock-on effect in the South with donors becoming increasingly questioning of traditional partners and the local NGOs consequently having to reassess themselves and their direction. It seems that established church partners who have benefited from institutional relations with church-related agencies, such as the Diocese of Sende, are particularly susceptible to such pressures.

Internal Factors
Changes in the external environment have a profound impact on internal aspects of the NGO. For example, external changes can often bring into question the organisation's very identity. They are no longer sure why they are doing what they are doing and yet, 'for organisations to determine and take hold of their own processes of change, they often need to be helped to become more conscious of their identity ... which is the life-force of an organisation – the very soul' (Taylor 1995).

NGO Growth and Development
Many NGOs have also been grappling with the particular issues which arise from rapid growth as well as development. As the TTO example most clearly shows (and the TUBA one to a lesser degree) organisations that grow quickly are faced with considerable pressures on the original leadership, the structure, the level of management skills (delegation, responsibility and authority, moni-

toring, breaking up of big tasks) required; the ownership and passion of the staff (sometimes with staff wanting more ownership of the organisation and leaders complaining that for the staff it was just a job). For many organisations this represents the common symptoms at the end of the 'pioneer phase' (or founders' phase). CDRA conclude that much of their OD work is *'around helping organisations deal with vision, leadership, and structural changes and systems and procedures involved in shifting an organisation from a Phase I to a Phase II organisation'* – a change illustrated by the NRDN case as well as some of the issues experienced in the Fellowship and CRC cases.

Addressing Issues of Poor Performance

The recognition of poor programme performance and limited impact (either through internal monitoring systems or external evaluations) has been another factor prompting these NGOs such as TTO, ABA and EWDFA to undergo a process of organisational change.

Internal Unrest

Closely related to factors involving poor performance and rapid growth is that of internal unrest. Poor programme performance and the lack of 'ownership' from new staff (and founders' unwillingness to let go) are often the major contributors to internal unrest. The TTO example powerfully demonstrates this dangerous cocktail. The EWDFA case also shows how a lack of impact quickly gave way to internal dissatisfaction and unrest.

A sense of alienation of the staff or members, even if it does not contribute significantly to internal unrest can be a factor in promoting an OD intervention.

What were the Main Triggers for the OD Interventions?
External Donors

European NGO donors played a key role in triggering some of the OD interventions described. In some cases such as Sende and ABA, the donors merely put it on the agenda as part of their ongoing relationship with the NGO. In another case, NRDN, the OD intervention was meant to be part of the donor's exit strategy (though this was resisted by the consultants and in fact never occurred). Despite its major limitations, trying to use OD or capacity-building as a sort of 'golden handshake' is quite popular with international NGOs facing very real issues of 'what do you do for partners you no longer want?'. A recent Oxfam letter to their partners, notifying them of budget cuts concluded, *'please inform us of any capacity-building we could provide to enable you to be in a better position to obtain funding from different sources'*. Financial crises often provoked by donor withdrawal or suspension of funding often force NGOs into change. More positively some donors, such as Bilance, are also using OD as an 'entry strategy', so that along with the first year's funding comes a grant for dealing with issues of strategy and direction as was the case with the TUBA example.

Internal Triggers

The OD interventions which have been presented are by no means all triggered by external pressure. We have seen particularly in the TTO and EWDFA cases that it was the internal recognition of problems (such as poor performance and staff unrest) which made them request the OD interventions.

Structural changes, such as the merger of two bodies, as in the Fellowship of Churches example, where it became essential to clarify the identity and role of the new one, can also be a trigger for change. The need to consciously manage the symptoms of growth (such as the division of roles and responsibilities and the development of internal systems) as in the case of CRC also trigger change processes. In addition, financial crises may not always be blamed on the suspension of donor funds; they may be due to poor management of existing funds (from which donors are not prepared to bail them out). The imperative for change is the same.

While OD consultants are usually brought in as a response to some form of perceived crisis, there are instances where OD consultants are brought in to preempt crises such as with the Fellowship of Churches and Olive. The Fellowship of Churches (and CRC) was not facing any undue crisis and used established systems of regular evaluation as the trigger for OD. Interestingly, but perhaps uniquely, the desire for one organisation to practise what it preaches in learning led Olive to institute annual OD exercises seeking outside support to be *'another pair of eyes, bringing a new perspective and constantly bringing us up to the mark'*.

What were the Key Entry Points for OD?
Programme Performance Evaluations

One of the clearest findings of the cases particularly from South Africa was the key role that evaluations often played as an entry point or even as a trigger to an OD intervention. *'They are an increasingly common starting-point which provide NGOs with time to take stock and review'* according to one consultant.

The NRDN case came out of a routine three-year evaluation and with the Fellowship of Churches 'the intervention was conceptualised as an evaluation'. The case study was written by the consultant in order to present the good use of an evaluation as a development tool. (In order to be involved in evaluations, however, CDRA define evaluations as a forward-looking process. Only if this is consistent with the client's view (the local NGO, not the donor) will they then go ahead.) With the CRC work it had been an evaluation which revealed the need for greater formalisation of job descriptions, but always implicit investigation of wider issues of independence. Olive state that every opportunity can be used to start off a whole systems approach stating that as a result *'we always workshop our evaluations'*.

One of the ongoing debates about NGO capacity-building is whether the capacity-building programmes focus so much on the internal organisational issues that they lose sight of the end product. Developing OD interventions on the basis of performance weaknesses demonstrates clearly how interrelated they are and how inseparable they should be.

Organisational Issues – Mission and Strategy

'OD TOOLS CAN CHALLENGE THE TRADITIONAL APPROACHES OF EVALUATION'

Not all the cases used programme evaluations as 'entry points ' for OD. Some interventions went straight into dealing with organisational issues. An increasingly common and useful entry point for OD work is organisations requesting support in developing their mission and long-term strategy. The most common entry point of the cases was at the level of vision, mission and strategy. The OD interventions with TUBA, EWDFA, ABA, Sende were all at this level.

Values and Culture

Some of the other cases began even 'deeper' at the level of values and culture. The TTO case in particular involved identifying the current organisational culture and developing a values statement describing the desired culture.

Systems

The CRC intervention used the development of job descriptions (a recommendation from a previous evaluation) as part of improving human resource systems as the way into dealing with issues of structure and even identity.

Training

Training is one of the often quoted entry points into OD. The need for staff training is an easily identified need and is popular with donors and NGOs. While problems are initially defined at the level of mere skills, it often becomes apparent that they are more deep-rooted and OD interventions then develop. If training is taken with a holistic view of organisations then this can foster deeper interventions (particularly as the client gets to know the trainers/consultants more). Interestingly, however, these particular cases do not yield much evidence for this. Certainly training was usually an integral part of OD intervention (or as part of follow-through), but did not actually provide the entry point.

What Types of Method were Used in the OD Interventions?

The majority of the OD interventions written up by the consultants as case studies are at a fairly deep level:

Vision, Mission, Values:	Sende; TTO
Mission and Strategy:	TUBA; ABA; Fellowship of Churches; NRDC; Olive
Strategic Planning and Programme Planning:	EWDFA
Systems and Structures (then identity):	CRC

What is clear from the cases is that an intervention on one level has an impact on many of the other levels. For example, the CRC intervention while seemingly at the level of systems and structures clearly had an impact on the culture and core of that particular part of the organisation as it moved from looking at job descriptions to dealing with the question of the department's identity as a separate organisation. Likewise, the work done at the heart of the organisation, in cases like Sende, obviously has an impact on issues of structure, skills and even resources.

How representative of common practice these interventions are is an open question. The selection of the case-study writers and their selection of the case study would suggest that these interventions are not 'normal'. 'Expert' organisational consultancies are much more common in the NGO sector than OD process consultancies, though for the CDRA who specialise in OD consultancies, much of their work is around:

- Visioning
- Mission-Building
- Leadership (Pioneer Counselling)
- Strategic Directions
- Structural Changes
- Systems Development (Monitoring and Evaluation, Personnel, Financial)
- Conflict Resolution
- Team-Building

By trying to plot the case studies using the typology of 'Major Families of OD

Interventions' we encountered in Chapter 2, we see how difficult it is to separate the focus of the intervention onto particular parts of the organisation. An intervention focusing on the whole organisation also has an impact on inter-group relations for example.

Individual	Team	Inter-group Relations	Total Organisation
ABA NRDC TTO	TUBA Olive Sende EWDFA	ABA TUBA Olive Fellowship of Churches EWFDA TTO Sende	TUBA ABA Olive Sende Fellowship of Churches NRDC TTO EWFDA

What also becomes clear from this analysis of the cases is that:

- they are almost all focused on the whole organisation (perhaps reflecting the relatively small size of most NGOs);
- the process-oriented ways in which these interventions were carried out at the total organisational level had a positive impact on intergroup relations, and team-building (again the small size of some NGOs makes it difficult to distinguish between the two);
- it was often necessary to do considerable work with top leadership at an individual level in order to make the OD intervention successful.

What Phases of OD Consultancy were Carried Out?
The OD processes used in most of the cases followed a fairly similar action research methodology and phases described in Chapter 2.

Contracting and Entry
What is clear from these examples of supposedly 'good practice' OD interventions is that the primary contract was between the consultant and the client, not with the donor. CDRA and EASUN, among others, have it as a non-negotiable condition that contracting must be done directly with the client and not with the donor. While this may appear very obvious common sense, the shocking aspect is that this is still not the norm with many other attempts at capacity-building of Southern NGOs.

Data Gathering

The primary data gathering methodology used by most of the cases was interviews with key stakeholders: most (if not all) of the staff; board members and trustees; beneficiaries and sometimes donors too. These interviews were most commonly semi-structured, though in the Olive case a more 'lightly' structured format was followed, letting key issues emerge from quite general and open-ended discussions. In all cases this was complemented by analysis of secondary, documentary sources and observation. Focus group discussions were also used and in some cases, such as TUBA and Sende a questionnaire was also a part of the process

Analysis and Feedback – Reporting

As we observed in Chapter 2, the critical issue for the success of the OD process is that the client 'owns' the analysis. The danger at this stage is for the consultant to present his or her findings in such a way that the client rejects them or sees them as someone else's. The cases show us different ways in which the consultants sought to avoid this problem.

The Feedback – Data Analysis Process

Some examples of typical processes are:

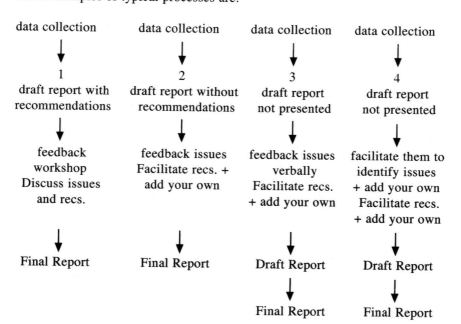

The cases analysed in this research can be broadly divided into these approaches:

2	3	4
TTO	Olive	TUBA
Fellowship of Churches		Sende
NRDN		EWDFA
		ABA

Which approach is taken obviously depends on a number of factors such as time available, the issues identified, and the client's demands. The rule of thumb is to follow the process which in your judgement will best facilitate organisational change. Interestingly, while most other consultants in the cases tended to withhold any written report until after the workshop, CDRA seem to prefer writing draft reports beforehand on the basis that *'difficult issues require a report to surface them before the workshop'*. Reports can give space for reflection and time to think about and to interpret the information. Their experience suggests that *'just having a workshop alone can generate shopping lists'*.

Certainly in the CDRA presented case studies, the reports had a big impact on the process, with clients commenting about it and forcing them to make the shift. CDRA often use these reports simply to mirror back and reflect what people are saying, and, as in the Triple Trust example, withholding any of the consultant's analysis and interpretation until later. They find that *'the draft report has unbelievable power if based on a reflection of what people say. Once something is committed to writing then it has a power of its own'*. Sometimes it would include some consultant's analysis too, *'you need to present them with a framework within which the chaos makes sense. This is what you told me; this is my reading of the issues'*. The report would then be used as a key diagnosis tool in designing the workshop to deal with the issues highlighted. In this case consultants' recommendations are limited to suggesting how the workshop should be designed, leaving recommendations for practical steps in organisational change to the workshop itself.

Reports do, however, have to be used with care and only if they are an effective tool in the whole process. The CDRA client who asserted the importance of the report in accelerating organisational change also said that the report almost pushed them to suicide!

The other major danger is that writing a report can remove the ownership of the issues from the client organisation and put the facilitator in the role of expert or even judge which is why the other case presenters tended to avoid them. According to van Boeschoten, 'I resist submitting a consultant's report – I try to get the client to write their own report on the situation. It will be far more important and in touch than any consultant's report' (CDRA 1996:13). Another consultant said that they only wrote reports if it was for an evaluation; *'if it were a strategic planning process such a report was often not necessary and could get in the way'.*

Workshops

While the reporting process was quite different, all of the interventions examined then had a workshop with staff (and sometimes board members) to jointly analyse the findings and think through the way forward. These workshops were much more than mere feedback meetings, but seen as strategic change intervention. They were very much at the heart of all the OD interventions. It was during these workshops that the issues which had been highlighted were grappled with and proved to be the critical points of the change process.

The workshops varied in length from just one day to two weeks. In all cases where the workshop was limited to one day, it was seen (with the benefit of hindsight) as much too short by both the client and the consultant. A one-week workshop was the most common and generally seen as an appropriate length of time to be away from the office. Residential workshops were thought to be much more effective than 'commuting' workshops.

Follow-up

The follow-up to the workshops and reports took various forms:

- immediate time back in the office;
- one-day visits after three and six months;
- training client staff in 'Facilitating OD' back in their organisations;
- signposting to other providers of appropriate training and consultancy;
- others had no direct follow-up with the onus on the client to get back in touch.

The lack of sufficient follow-up was one of the main criticisms of the interventions looked at, with clients usually seeing the consultants as 'too busy' and sometimes without the resources to contract them further. Consultants are very aware of the dangers of creating dependency and therefore strive to ensure that the client is equipped to take responsibility for its own development. The consultants interviewed were also very aware that ethically they had to keep within the briefs they were given. Unless they were invited back, they could not force their way even if they thought it necessary. These very real concerns are reinforced by most consultants being extremely over-worked and faced with a plethora of other organisations demanding their limited time as well as with needing boundaries as a vital self-protection mechanism.

Some relationships between consultants and clients do have continuity and follow-though and many of the case studies presented in this publication lasted over a number of years and have moved on, since they were written, with further consultant contact. TUBA, for example, have just asked the consultant back after nine months to help them 'harden' their strategic directions into concrete programme plans. CDRA have relationships with clients lasting over ten years.

There seems to be an inherent tension between giving sufficient follow-through and yet avoiding dependence. It seems very hard to get the right balance, particularly in dynamic situations of organisation change when 'dependence' is at times a healthy part of the process. As the Olive case with CRC showed, it is important for consultants to constantly reassess their roles to discern where the imbalance is.

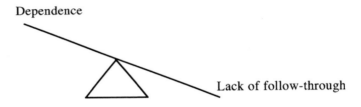

Harrison describes the balance as 'realistic dependence as distinguished from the dependence built into a patriarchal or hierarchical culture. Realistic dependency gives support and direction to empower others' (1995b:172).

How Long did the OD Interventions Last?

The overall amount of time which consultants spent with the clients on the OD interventions varied from a minimum of about 20 or so days (such as TUBA) to others such as Sende or EWDFA which involved well over 60 days. The 'length' of the OD processes described in the cases also varied from about nine months to three years. This shows that most of the cases fulfilled the criterion that OD processes should not be one-shot only solutions, but should be ongoing change programmes. Usually the same consultants were used throughout the OD process, though in the CRC case, CDRA were used to set the overall process moving in the whole organisation and then Olive were contracted to follow up with the intervention within the CRC department. Olive were seen to be better able to deliver on the specific improvements in human resource systems, as well as being much more geographically accessible. This shows how change should be a continuous process within agencies rather than a particular event or an intervention. In the case of CRC, the switch did not cause any significant dislocation as CDRA and Olive are *'collegiate organisations aware of each other's mode of thinking'*.

How did the OD Consultancies Relate to other Methods of Capacity-Building?

Training and OD consultancy are at best mutually supportive functions. At worst they are confused with one another to the extent that training interventions are applied inappropriately and ineffectively to situations which call for a consultative intervention and vice versa ... Training may be a part of OD when the goals of OD indicate a need to help people develop skills or competencies that would facilitate movement towards desired goals or changes. (Hanson and Lubin 1995:44)

OD consultancy is just one method for building the capacity of organisations. It is dangerous to become too intoxicated with it in isolation. There are many other capacity-building approaches including training, South-South exchanges, dialogue, structured demonstrations, secondments, as well as providing resources. These approaches to capacity-building are NOT mutually exclusive, but more often than not are mutually reinforcing and should be used together as a coherent and systematic approach. Complex organisational problems are unlikely to be solved by just a single approach and there is no one right way for all situations. As one respondent commented, *'OD and training feed into each other. To bring about a real shift new understanding is needed which may need a variety of different methodologies'*.

Many OD processes start off as a request for training. Problems are initially defined at the level of skills, but in fact they are often more deep-rooted. As trust is built up and as underlying issues are uncovered, OD processes often develop. For example, the Olive training of CRC coordinators was developed and reinforced by their subsequent involvement in looking at the whole independence of the CRCs. As well as being an entry point, training is often an integral part of an ODC intervention as we saw in the NRDC case and the CRC case in particular where *'people needed to be trained in their new roles and responsibilities in this different structure'*. Training and OD consultancy were seen to be *'mutually enriching and reinforcing'* and Sende was able to support the OD work by sending the coordinator on a CORAT course in 'Understanding Development'.

Training may also be used to deal with content issues which the OD provider does not specialise in. One consultant said, for example, *'management skills are important, we all know that and being able to refer allows me to concentrate (on OD consultancy)'*.

Training is also commonly used as a follow-through of an OD consultancy process. The CDRA training course entitled 'Facilitating OD' has been primarily used by CDRA as a means for following-up their OD consultancy interventions by training 2–3 key members of a client organisation in order to effectively implement the change process after CDRA have left, such as was seen by the 'Fellowship of Churches' case study, and its absence was lamented by Triple Trust (though people were sent on a PACT course). EASUN in Tanzania are putting on the very same course (in conjunction with CDRA) also as an entry point (or marketing tool) for prospective clients to understand what OD is about, to develop more East African OD advisers, and to follow through on some of their existing OD work such as with ABA.

A further linkage between training and OD consultancy is that the *'OD process is training for staff itself. It has trained them to go into communities more effectively'.*

Other capacity-building interventions such as exchange visits have been used by organisations like CRC to support the OD work on independence.

Where were These Consultants Based – can They be within Agencies?

The cases presented are all examples of external OD providers, though an example of an internal OD intervention was sought in vain. The advantages of using external consultants was highlighted by many respondents. As has been noted one of the NGOs tried to be its own doctor and failed badly as *'heart values and culture are very hard to diagnose and fix on your own. Trust was quite an issue covering many different elements of diversity'.* Outsiders have no agenda and can be more impartial so *'it is easier to feel safe with an outsider when there are very painful, conflictive issues'.* In addition one agency mentioned the benefits of an outside consultant being that *'their presence forces reflection to happen'.* These responses reinforce the view of French and Bell, that 'organisations are better served by outside OD specialists who are free from the constraints or organisational culture and who can take a more neutral role in working with members of the organisation' (1984:20).

To some degree, the internal/external debate is beside the point as there are complementary roles to play. A successful OD process needs to be driven from within even if an external consultant is used and the critical goal of an external OD consultant is to develop the capacity within the organisation to carry on change. It is not a question of either/or but ensuring that it is both/and.

Should Consultants Work in Teams or Alone?

One of the similarities in most of the cases is how the OD interventions were carried out by teams of consultants, usually in pairs, rather than by individuals. In this way the consultant teams were able to bring greater diversity (gender, race, nationality), experience, expertise as well as an ability to play different roles and provide a sounding board for each other. Not surprisingly it is part of most providers' strategies to try and undertake work in teams rather than individually as *'it increases the quality while reducing the risk, as well as bringing in others for their own development'*.

One case in particular illustrated the value of the OD provider putting together the team. The clients themselves said, *'the experience made me wonder at the value of bringing in teams. It depends on who selects the team. If they are selected by the client then they can be cumbersome as they have never worked together and might not have chosen each other'*. The lead consultant agreed that this team did not work well, in his opinion, *'the most important knowledge is that which exists within the organisation itself'*.

Chapter 5

The Impact of ODC and Key Success Factors

INTRODUCTION

Having looked at how the OD processes took place in practice, it is now important to investigate whether in fact these processes did have any impact on the organisations on the receiving end and whether any of these benefits trickled down to community level. The cases provide rich evidence of this as well as clearly pointing out some of the key factors in making some OD consultancies more effective and others less effective. Some of the critical NGO questions addressed in this chapter are:

- Does ODC work?
- What is the impact at the level of beneficiaries?
- What were the key success factors in these OD interventions?
- At what stage of growth are NGOs more amenable to ODC?
- Did the type of organisation matter?
- Were there any major differences in the OD processes with church organisations compared to secular ones?
- In what contexts was ODC an appropriate approach?
- What OD strategy is appropriate in situations of conflict?

THE IMPACT OF ODC

Does ODC Work?

The European NGOs interviewed at the start of this research were unable to be categorical as to the impact of the OD consultancy they had supported. Some agencies believed it had been quite effective while others were not so sure. While they all thought it was vital to know whether OD made any difference to poverty alleviation and if so what sort of correlation existed, very few had much evidence on which to base their judgements. Partly this lack of information arose from the Southern NGO being 'the client' in the intervention and the Northern NGO sometimes being left out of the reporting feedback loop. Other times it arose because the evidence was at best anecdotal and based on individual perceptions (for example in one agency where two staff were interviewed about exactly the same intervention, they came to opposite conclusions about its value!). The case study research was designed to shed some light on this area.

The methodology used for evaluating the impact involved interviews with a number of different stakeholders in the OD process including where possible:

- the consultant;
- the NGO director;
- a cross-section of 2–3 NGO staff members;
- some beneficiaries (although resource constraints made this limited);
- the donor.

The case studies presented go some way to providing evidence that OD consultancy can have an impact on strengthening the capacity of NGOs. This evidence from just nine case studies, however, does not allow extrapolation to say that OD consultancy always has a positive impact – merely that if it is done well in appropriate conditions then it has the potential. These findings are reinforced by the experience of African OD providers too. An external evaluation of CDRA in 1993 concluded 'CDRA has had a major impact on civil society by building a viable, effective and coherent consultancy practice' (1993/4:21) and 'EASUN's experience shows that clients who have experienced what OD can bring to the well-being of an organisation were enthusiastic to ask for further interventions' (EASUN 1996a:3). Most OD providers tend to have fairly limited systems to date for measuring the impact of their work.

ORGANISATIONAL CHANGE

INDIVIDUAL CHANGE

COMMUNITY CHANGE

ODC IMPACT ROCKET

WHAT IS THE IMPACT OF ODC?

We shall examine the cases in terms of the:

- internal outcomes (the organisation and individuals);
- external outcomes (the community);
- OD process itself.

Internal Outcomes
Organisational Changes
Given those qualifications there was significant evidence from the cases studies examined that organisational change had taken place as a result of the OD interventions.

Very Existence and Survival
It was clear from four of the case studies that the OD interventions had contributed to the NGO's very survival. Respondents from Triple Trust, ABA and the Fellowship of Churches all claimed that without the OD intervention they were unsure whether the organisation would exist at all today. The fact that TUBA is still functioning despite the absence of a director for the last 11 months as well as the departure of the four most senior members of staff can be partially attributed to the broadening of the ownership of the organisation through the strategic planning process. It should be recognised, however, that dying needs to take place in an organisation and sometimes the most positive 'developmental' step is for an organisation to die, especially as this often enables new energy and new initiatives to emerge, as in the case of ABA. As Smith says, 'OD specialists do have a role in helping organisations to die with dignity' (1997).

Ability to Take on its own Change Process
Many of the interventions indicated that facilitating the NGO to take charge of its own development had been achieved to a certain extent. For example in the CRC case it was noted that *'the CRCs now want to get on and implement change, not*

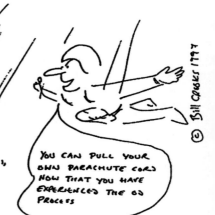

You can pull your own parachute cord now that you have experienced the OD process

© Bill Crooks 1997

just talk about it. The momentum is now there'. One reason for the lack of follow-through at Triple Trust was due to senior management's belief that sufficient structures had been put in place to enable them to solve their own problems (though this was disputed by some middle-managers).

Other noticeable changes in organisational capacity were identified by the case studies:

Values and Culture

Organisational culture was obviously affected by many of the OD interventions. A number of clients noted *'enormous shifts in culture'*. With NRDN the pioneer culture gave way to a more differentiated and delegated way of working. The EWDFA consultant stated that *'despite the military culture which pervaded at the start, decision-making has become more consultative and decentralised with regular meetings formalised'*. In Sende too, the OD intervention was seen to counter the dominant cultures of dualism and passivity with the OD process contributing to the whole 'indigenisation of the church' as vision and direction were being set by African lay people. For Olive the process was seen to reinforce their reflective culture, while for Triple Trust tangible aspects like a values statement was developed to describe the type of culture in which staff wanted to operate.

Identity and Mission

Dealing with issues of identity was a common theme in many of the cases and evidence of development in this area is plentiful. ABA and the Sende Development office both thought that the process enabled them for the first time to know what they were doing and why. Similarly with the Fellowship of Churches a major part of the intervention was helping the client to conceptualise what they are trying to bring to the world, with the workshop leading to a *'real paradigm shift'* and a new mission statement to reflect that. For EWDFA and Sende the OD processes led to vision and mission statements being produced.

Strategy

Strategic plans and programme plans produced were products of the OD interventions with TUBA, EWDFA (and Sende soon) and strategic planning processes were introduced elsewhere. These are obviously visible manifestations of the intent to change. More importantly, the OD interventions resulted in very real changes in strategy with programmes being closed down. For TUBA this meant they had to say 'no' to implementing a World Bank project as well as phase out of a donor-led implementation project. For NRDN and the Fellowship of

Churches they too phased out of or handed over some major projects which were outside their new strategy.

The OD interventions helped many of the clients think and act more strategically. For Olive and Sende it returned 'focus' to the organisation and for the CRCs they were *'now able to think beyond the present 14 centres to what we should do in the future'*.

Systems and Structures

Structural changes are also some of the more visible aspects of organisational change. For NRDN, Triple Trust and the Fellowship of Churches obvious structural changes took place such as the creation of full-time posts for finance and the establishment of management committees. Clear roles and responsibilities were developed during some of the OD interventions thus easing the load and pressure on the leaders. For Sende too it was recognised that the fragmented structure had been improved by integrating the development office with the rest of the organisation.

In addition many of the processes also encouraged the adoption of new systems, such as personnel, finance and planning. While these have been definitely introduced and documented, they have usually been triggered but not always done by the OD consultants. With Sende, though, the consultants have helped develop the financial systems and Olive have helped the Fellowship of Churches with human resource management systems.

People

While it is easier to see changes in the more formal elements of organisation, the OD consultancies also brought significant changes in the vital 'people'-related areas. At the level of leadership, it was seen on more than one occasion to have *'saved the director from burn-out'* with one leader saying that it was *'very helpful for me personally to narrow focus, releasing me from a feeling that we had to respond to everything'*. It also meant in other cases such as TTO that *'there were immediate changes in the leadership with a desire to be more consultative'* or with ABA that the intervention radically altered the behaviour and attitude of the leadership. It also sometimes strengthened the leadership by involving the board in the OD process which challenged them to be more involved in the organisation.

For staff there were considerable changes in terms of

– skills

With EWDFA, evaluations gave evidence of enhanced skills and with NRDN the *'level of analysis and depth of questions increased dramatically becoming able to critique and change their own practice'.*

– relationships
Progress was also made in the area of relationships with internal conflict handled positively in ABA, Triple Trust and in EWDFA where *'civilians are happier with combatant colleagues'.*

– motivation
In order for staff to be motivated they need to have an understanding of 'why are we here' for *'if people understand how their work fits with the overall objectives of the organisation, then massive energy is released'* according to one consultant. Enhancing staff ownership of the organisation and thereby increasing motivation occurred in a few of the cases including, Triple Trust, ABA and TUBA.

Without any outside prompting, there are many ways the recipients of these interventions have articulated for themselves the impact of the OD consultancies. The OD interventions have been written about as bringing key changes by the organisations themselves in their newsletters and annual reports. Internally too the changes are evident. For Triple Trust *'it is a key point in our history, we speak about the CDRA event'* and others lament, *'I always felt a little robbed not being part of the workshop. It seemed to be a crucial event which changed the life of the organisation'.*

The providers of OD services have also noticed the changes in the external relations of the NGO with their donors and consultants as *'the terms of reference for the next job were much better and the nature and depth of the questions had moved on'.*

One further interesting indicator that the OD consultancies were effective is that two of the organisations on the receiving end have since developed OD consultancy services of their own – imitation being the sincerest form of flattery. The NRDN leader is now able to give support to others in OD and Triple Trust having developed their own OD provision-wing, the Institute of Development Services.

Individual Level
While it is clear that OD consultancy can have a significant impact on the client organisation, possibly the greatest impact is at the level of the individuals involved as *'the real value of these processes is the individual learning that takes place'.* With the ABA case, the main impact of the OD process so far is to help the organisation die to its old self, but the *'individual learning ... hopes and ideas remain'* with the expectation that this will enable something new and bet-

ter to arise. According to one respondent, *'in terms of what people are able to do now as a result of experiencing the intervention may be very different and may have an impact throughout their lives with all the different organisations they work with, not just this present one'*. Even the least positive commentator about the long-term impact of the work with Triple Trust stated *'we learnt lots of things in that workshop which we now know and use. The process was very empowering for me individually. It crystallised a lot of things and gave rise to massive individual learning'*.

What is the Impact at the Level of Beneficiaries?

External Outcomes

Changes at Community Level

Many people, however, are not just content to support changes which strengthen the organisation itself. For many capacity-building is only a means to an end of greater impact at community level.

Certainly the changes are much more visible at an organisational level as *'most of the changes occur in the office rather than the field'*. The impact is more indirect at a community level and may not even be immediately visible or

"THE RIPPLE EFFECT"

understood at that level. While to some this meant that the impact of the intervention on the ultimate beneficiaries was *'negligible'* to others the indirect effect was still very real as *'change has a ripple effect outwards'*.

Having staff better trained and motivated certainly would improve the impact at the grass-roots level of beneficiaries. As with the Fellowship of Churches, it was seen that the intervention had a significant impact at community level as *'staff are now trained to do work'* and with Triple Trust the effect was experienced *'through fieldworkers feeling part of the organisation'*.

Certainly too if an organisation is suffering from severe organisational problems then this will be a significant constraint on their effectiveness, such as with Triple Trust who were paralysed for one year before the OD intervention and with the Fellowship of Churches, whose staff *'were overstretched and stressed and not performing optimally'*. Addressing these organisational ills, therefore, will have a very real impact on beneficiaries.

The OD engagements also had direct impact in terms of the programme methodologies. They have sometimes enabled communities to be more directly involved in the planning of projects. For the Fellowship of Churches, it meant *'communities were involved in the planning process for the first time'* and *'the CRCs have become much more a part of the community not just us'*. For the Diocese of Sende there was *'the expectation that the process would help us find out whether our work was the priority of the people. Now we are sure the demands come from the people'*. The OD process for Sende also promoted the participation of women and youth for the first time with the result that they now feel part of the church. Also, changes in attitude have been noted with people no longer just waiting for handouts from the church but instead, taking responsibility for their own development.

Evaluating the OD Process

The OD process can also be evaluated itself in a number of ways:

After the workshop element of most OD processes, there is immediate feedback from the participants which tends to be fairly positive, but does not give much of an indication about actual changes which will take place in the organisation.

More telling is whether the action plans developed during the OD intervention have actually been implemented back in the organisation. There is evidence from some certainly that this has been carried out – the Fellowship of Churches stating that *'we have set in motion all the recommendations from the process except for salary structures which we will do in the first half of this year'*.

Some of the OD providers undertook their own external evaluations of the process some months after the intervention (as opposed to or in addition to proving further follow-up), with specific meetings taking place to review the process. This was seen both by clients and by the providers as being of great value, without which some of the lingering issues might not be dealt with.

Another way of evaluating the success of an intervention is by monitoring the clients' reaction through letters, phone calls and further contact. CDRA have a 'brag' book of positive letters after interventions (as well as an organisational learning book of critical feedback). One of the case study clients said, *'we use CDRA for on-going advice. Only last week we rang them up to find out what they thought were the pros and cons of staff committees'*.

The ultimate measure of whether a client thinks that the intervention has been cost-effective is whether they invite the consultant back for further work. The CDRA intervention with the Fellowship of Churches was the second time they had been specifically involved; Dave Harding has now been to Olive three times; Olive themselves have undertaken a number of interrelated interventions with the CRCs of the Fellowship of Churches. CDRA have some ongoing relationships with clients which stretch over ten years. The converse can also be a measure of effectiveness being 'the number of times people refuse to pay'.

While control groups are notoriously difficult in development, the CDRA case with Triple Trust does allow a comparison of 'with and without OD consultancy'. Before the very positive reaction to the CDRA work, Triple Trust tried to be their *'own doctor'* which only resulted in *'greater frustration and paralysis'*.

A final way of measuring the process is to gauge the extent to which it is owned by the organisation. Again the case studies provide evidence for this, for according to ABA, *'the process was very good. It got the information and the ideas from the people. It was our product'* or as Sende put it *'what they came out with was ours, not theirs'*.

KEY SUCCESS FACTORS IN INTERVENTIONS

What were the Key Success Factors in these OD Interventions?
The key success factors in the OD case studies can be usefully divided into six broad areas:

- ownership of the need for change;
- the consultancy process;
- the consultants themselves;
- of the donor/NGO relationship;
- the nature of the NGO;
- the wider context.

Ownership in the NGO
Ownership

The prime factor determining the success or otherwise of an OD intervention mentioned by almost every respondent throughout the research was that the NGO itself owned the change process. NGOs had to have a felt need for change and be prepared to make their own investment of considerable time, effort and resources in the process. The cases demonstrate this clearly, with many of them paying for workshop costs and consultant fees themselves. In the words of one client, *'we paid for it ourselves initially ... if you do not do it yourself, you do not take it as seriously'.* There were also considerable non-financial costs which clients had to bear: *'little did we know how tough it is. It is taking a massive amount of time and extra effort and frustration on our part with a high personal cost on our children'.* As an example of this commitment, one respondent from this organisation voluntarily travelled 210 km just to be interviewed by the author about his views on the OD process.

OWNERSHIP BY THE CLIENT OF THE PROCESS IS VITAL

The ownership of the change process is closely related to how keenly the NGO perceives the need. Unless key people in the organisation feel the need for change none is likely to occur. For NGOs such as Triple Trust or ABA they believed the situation to be so desperate that they had no choice and so the onus on change was high. For EWDFA too it was thought that the organisation had reached a point of crisis with increasing internal conflict and stagnant programmes.

Conditions need to exist which preclude the maintenance of the status quo. For organisations really to take on the tensions and effort of change and overcome the inherent resistances it must be clear that not changing would be even more dangerous and threatening. In the ABA case, for example, the consultant used 'future scenario' tools to reveal the massive cost of doing nothing. Kotter, in his classic work said that for a change process to succeed 75% of management must be honestly convinced that business as usual is unacceptable (1995:62). Respondents thought that it was necessary to have a sense of urgency with the organisation 'in pain, but not too much pain' – facing a **'moderate' crisis!** If the crisis, however, was too acute, then more immediate (and coercive) approaches might be more appropriate.

Two of the OD cases (Olive and the Fellowship of Churches), however, are with NGOs at points of relative stability rather than crisis. While the change process may have been owned as much by these two organisations, perhaps the extent of their actual change was less.

The cases did reveal the value of having both internal and external pressures for change. Internal pressures for change were important to ensure peoples' commitment as shown by TUBA, Sende, Triple Trust and EWDFA's recognition of their own weaknesses and dissatisfaction with their current performance. These internal pressures are often articulated in staff feelings that they are constantly firefighting; overstretched; and unable to meet beneficiary demands; and seen in low staff morale and increasing staff turnover.

While these internal pressures are essential, more frequently the required 'crisis' is actually triggered by external factors such as negative donor evaluations and 'doubts over resources' such as was seen with Sende. The moment the funding future is less secure, then suddenly NGOs become more open to change. Some respondents even thought that *'funding insecurity is a precondition for change'*! If there are already sufficient internal pressures for change (a felt need) then it does not seem to be a problem that external factors trigger the change process. This external trigger can be likened to a match which will be effective in lighting a fire only if kindling is already there. If there are no such internal pressures, the match will burn brightly, but quickly fizzle and die.

The level of ownership of a change programme is closely correlated with the nature of leadership support. While some change initiatives might have come from the staff, unless the leadership supported these change efforts or came to support them, it appeared they were doomed to fail. Almost all the cases described the critical role of leadership in driving the change process. Leadership acceptance is not enough – their positive energies are essential for its success. As one of the consultants in the case studies reported,

> The organisation did shift, the conflict was resolved – in part because leadership made unbelievable changes – and the entire strategy changed ... leaders often have to go through the most major changes, which often means letting go of past perceptions which is difficult. If leadership can't shift, then no organisational process can succeed. (Kaplan 1995:2)

Leaders have to have an understanding of the need for change, the emotional acceptance of that change and the will to implement it in their organisations and with themselves. The leadership must also have ownership of the process, not just the need for change. The ABA case benefited from the 'fascination' the leader had with the OD process itself. The case studies also reveal that ownership and top management commitment are not static phenomena. In the example of Sende, leadership commitment was not really there at the start, but it was the process itself that brought this. Other case studies such as TTO or NRDN mentioned 'a moment of truth' for the leadership well into the OD process – the will of the organisation sometimes needs to be **woken**.

Staff Involvement and Ownership

There also needs to be individual ability and willingness of staff throughout the organisation to make changes. Organisational change is as much a political or social process as it is technical. A critical mass of support is therefore necessary with key change agents at different points in the organisation. Powerful coalitions need to be formed with enough power within the organisation to manage the change process. Identifying key opinion leaders (or will carriers) is a common and effective part of many approaches to change (this is called the Shaka Strategy in South Africa). One of the key factors in the success of the CRC process was the existence of key change agents within the CRC programme as well as having the full-time commitment of a powerful staff member. In the EWDFA example we noted that the organisation had the advantage that the combatants had extremely strong team spirit. They were used to working together. They had been sharing their beliefs, pain and dreams for many years.

Ultimately the effectiveness of the actual implementation of any change will largely depend on how the staff view the changes (or even other stakeholders like the priests at Sende). If key stakeholders are not involved little will change in practice, which is why for effective change one consultant said *'you need a culture of openness which should be built in from the start'* – the nature of the intervention process itself therefore was seen as crucial.

The Intervention Process

As well as ensuring that the need for change is clearly owned by the organisation, the cases indicate that design and implementation of the intervention process itself had an impact on the effectiveness of the work.

The principles of good practice in implementing OD processes which emerge from the cases are that they need to be **participatory**. To ensure staff ownership of the change process, their involvement in the intervention was seen as vital. The cases all described participative processes (though to differing degrees and at different points). For example, in the CRC case, *'staff were involved throughout the process',* and others commented on how the participative workshops had *'built trust and recognition'*. The participative workshop aspect of the OD interventions was seen as critical in enhancing staff ownership of both the needs and the solutions, and the danger of curtailing this part of the process was clearly seen in the Olive case.

The OD processes needed to be given enough **time**. Again and again, the importance of giving the process sufficient time was noted by clients, consultants and even some donors: *'we need to slow the pace of change down because* *to get real depth and quality you need time'*. People were aware of the danger that *'we are always in such a hurry to see results that we spoil the process'*. The NRDN case exemplifies an incremental approach which starts from where people are and goes at a pace which can be coped with, as otherwise *'it is very draining to do too much organisational change too quickly'*. One of the strengths of the Sende example is that *'it has gone at peoples' own pace'*. Kotter puts it clearly when he says that 'the change process goes through a series of phases that in total usually require a considerable length of time. Skipping steps creates only the illusion of speed' (Kotter 1995).

At the same time, the importance of losing momentum should not be ignored as in the case of ABA where much of the energy for the change process was dissipated over time.

Closely related to giving the process sufficient time was the need to develop a **flexible and an intermittent process**. One consultant described OD as *'an unfolding process where you cannot know everything at the beginning. You have to start outside and work towards the heart'*. The NRDN and CRC cases are a good example of flexible, integrated processes which occurred at periodic moments over a number of years.

The cases also illustrate the OD principle of assessing the **whole organisation** and seeing the interrelated elements, including the board. Part of the problem with the TUBA case is that when the director and chair of the board left, other board members had not been part of the process. The Sende example too showed how it is important for church-based organisations to overcome the dualistic pastoral/development division and to work with the whole organisation to effect meaningful change.

OD processes benefited from understanding the political dimensions of organisations. For example, the Sende case showed the need to **identify political 'power points'** in organisations and to work with an internal group with sufficient political weight.

The OD interventions in the cases were thought to be more effective if there was sufficient **follow-through** and the need for this should be discussed at the initial stage of contracting for the consultancy to ensure that both the client and the consultant allow enough time for this. The 1993 evaluation of CDRA showed that the agencies which had benefited most were those who had had an ongoing relationship with the CDRA.

Clear plans with indictors and bench-marks also strengthened the OD interventions where definite time schedules with roles and responsibilities were allocated. One of the case study clients noted *'we have set plans and goals to implement changes'*. There needs to be constant monitoring of the change process, as well as designing it to allow for 'short-term wins' (some quick, visible results to motivate staff further).

The cases also showed the benefit of using a **variety of change strategies.** Training was used as a key complement to consultancy in many of the cases, including NRDC, Sende, Fellowship of Churches and CRC.

The Consultants

The nature of the OD process designed obviously is inextricably linked with the person designing it. The critical importance of the skills, knowledge and attitudes of the consultants emerged clearly from the cases and reinforces the qualities highlighted in Chapter 2.

Consultants had to **quickly build a relationship of confidence and trust** with the NGO if the intervention was to work. This obviously helps if consultants have worked with clients over a period time and can help if clients have the impression that, as one client said, *'he knows us better than we know our own pockets'*. The consultant in the EWDFA case knew the importance of gaining the disabled fighters' trust in overcoming the resistance to him as an able-bodied civilian, so put in a lot of background preparation to understand the history of the struggle in Eritrea as well as other African liberation struggles.

BUILDING RELATIONSHIPS WITH THE CLIENT IS VITAL FOR AN EFFECTIVE OD CONSULTING PROCESS

Consultants also employed **appropriate consulting styles** and had well-developed personal skills to lead clients through very sensitive and at times conflictive processes. The NRDN case showed how different 'confrontational and acceptant' consulting styles were used to great effect in such circumstances. Another consultant in the Fellowship of Churches was described by the client as having a *'very people-friendly style'* and that he was *'the best person who has ever worked with the Fellowship of Churches in all the time I have been here'*.

The case studies revealed the importance of consultants having **well-developed communication skills.** They benefited from good verbal communication skills in the mother tongue of the client group. The problems of having translators was mentioned in the EWDFA case and even with ABA. Despite the consultant being a national, it was felt that communication difficulties hindered a free flow between participants and the facilitator. Conversely with Sende, the client noted that the consultant was able to *'speak the language of the people, not just the development office'*. Yet language ability alone is not enough as *'effective communication required a profound interpretation of cultural imagery and metaphor'* according to one consultant. As Geoff Mamputa puts it: 'the issue is finding the common ground and context from which we can communicate and work together' (1997:7). The importance of good written communication skills was also obvious from the cases. The CRC client stated that *'the reports of Olive were very helpful. They were thorough and accessible with prompt clear recommendations and conclusions'*.

Consultants also needed to have the analytical ability, experience and insight to **understand the reality of the client**, especially the local NGO context and values. While it was felt this might be easier if the consultant was from the same country, *'as it is easy for foreigners to misunderstand behaviour and cultural cues'*, this was clearly not a sufficient condition. The TTO example showed the advantages of having local external consultants with insight and experience to hold up a 'critical mirror' of the prevailing culture of the organisation. The need to understand the particular realities that each organisation faced also emerged in the Sende case where the second group of consultants appreciated the church context.

As well as knowing the local NGO context, the OD consultant needed to have a good sense of the **wider picture**, to see how the world is changing and how this might affect the NGO concerned. The benefit of having someone on the consultancy team in Sende who understood the perspective of the Northern NGO donors was often mentioned.

The cases also revealed the importance of the **consultants' attitude and approach** in giving inputs in such a way that the process of OD can be guided from within. One client responded that *'we were surprised by their approach which made us think for ourselves and so what we came out with was ours not* *theirs. We expected them to assist us to get what we want to do, instead they have guided us to think what we want to do'*. Others mentioned the importance of the consultants challenging them, saying, *'they kept reminding us that we could not abdicate responsibility. They kept putting us back in the driving seat'* and sometimes even said to them, *'I wonder if you will really do this. This must be your decision otherwise nothing will change'*.

Good consultants have to be **clear about their briefs, roles and boundaries.** The CRC case demonstrated the need to analyse regularly the roles the consultants played and renegotiate them as appropriate. As the client said, *'Olive has been very careful to get a clear sense of their brief and been very sensitive in checking back. I do not feel either organisation exceeded its mandate. Both (Olive and CDRA) were very thorough and cautious about the brief and if anything underplay their role to ensure our ownership'*.

The **availability of the consultants** was a very real issue. While one client commented, *'every time I had a problem his doors were open. I frequently stopped him in the centre of town as he was driving along'* another lamented that, *'they do not have enough time for us ... they are difficult to get hold of'* and feared being left in mid-air.

Relationship and Northern NGO Role

The existing relationship between the donor and the NGO also had a very real impact on the success or otherwise of the intervention. There is a danger that OD is driven by well-meaning donors, but *'there is a huge difference between working with clients who really want it and those who have it forced upon them'*. As Mosi Kisare has highlighted, 'much of the criticism of OD by NGOs was influenced by a context in which certain conditions are imposed by the North on the South' ... and goes on to point out that sometimes 'those who attempt to impose OD ... are misusing and abusing the discipline of OD for the sake of the imposition of their agenda' (1996:4). He warns of the danger of OD becoming another basis for conditionality and unwarranted intrusion into the affairs of African NGOs, noting that when a donor's project-driven needs are linked to an OD process then it certainly becomes an external agenda and cannot be successful in promoting the organisation development of NGOs (which is why so many external evaluations of NGOs contribute so little to important change processes).

The cases show that an obvious, but critical factor in this relationship is whether the Northern NGOs are prepared to **fund the OD process from a distance**. OD consultancy is expensive and not very 'donor appealing', but those agencies which had been able to access support for their OD processes such as Triple Trust, Olive, Sende greatly appreciated the role the donor had played in supporting the process financially. In the TUBA example too, the donor was flexible enough to let TUBA direct and contract the consultancy process. Their long-term view of a funding relationship with TUBA enabled TUBA to lengthen its strategic perspective. There is also a need for donors to be prepared to see these processes through and not withdraw support for the OD process when the quick-fix does not materialise. It was believed by Southern respondents that for OD to be effective, Northern NGOs had to stand alongside partners at difficult and 'unattractive' times, *'accepting failures as long as it had an overall positive trend'* and accepting slow change. OD needs adequate resources to support and maintain the change which is why it is such a poor 'exit strategy'.

As well as funding, the cases show that the Northern NGO donors also had an important role in **putting OD on the agenda** in the first place. One client responded *'someone has to trigger the idea. Usually it will come from the outside. Often money is involved as money makes people think'*. Sende described a positive dialogue with their donor in which *'the idea (for OD) originated from the donor, but was then taken up by the diocese'*. ABA also stated that they would not even have started without the assistance of the donor.

The dilemma is how to trigger process and then stand back and let the process move on its own.

In one of the cases, the donor lost its way a bit and tried to push and direct the process too much, *'deadlines were fixed by the donor which put us under great pressure which was not compatible with the participative process we wanted and the size and poor communications in the diocese. The donor ignored our involvement in pastoral activities'*. Donors can impose arbitrary time limits which do not take into account the local context or the nature of organisational change. Some donors even can be tempted to direct the change process themselves, as in one of the cases, by trying to force the organisation to fire a staff member through making it a funding conditionality. For consultants, *'it is very difficult to operate as the agent of the funder. People feel coerced and do not see the need themselves'*. The result is that *'OD is less successful in Africa because it is perceived as a Northern donor agenda'*. OD may become so linked to resources that it becomes another required funding hoop and not an approach to strengthen the organisation. Just as consultants have to determine clearly 'who is the client', so too do donors. There is the tendency for Northern donors to identify capacity-building needs in terms of what directly affects them: monitoring and evaluation; financial systems; proposal and report writing. In this case, whose needs is the capacity-building primarily serving?

Yet it was seen in the cases that donors should not be isolated from the OD process either as *'if they had been more involved in the process they would understand it better and be more supportive of what is going on'*. More significantly, NGOs do not operate in a vacuum, but as part of an open aid system. Donors may well be both a part of the problem and a part of the solution. OD processes which excluded a critical review of the relationships with Northern NGOs were seen as compartmentalising and superficial. Yet this involvement must be appropriate. In the EWDFA example the donor did not participate in early workshops as it would have been very tempting for the donor to move the process too quickly. At subsequent workshops they were able to be a bit more involved as the organisation was beginning to establish its identity. They could offer their views more constructively once the NGO's confidence had been gained.

The Nature of the NGO

One of the findings from these cases is the inverse relationship between the need for the intervention and the effectiveness of the OD intervention as a solution. To a limited degree with the CRC case it is clear that the very organisational weaknesses (the paternalistic management style of key staff) which necessitated the OD intervention in the first place then served to constrain the effectiveness of the consultancy. As Schein says, 'sick organisations tend to resist help' (1988:193).

At what Stage of Growth are NGOs More Amenable to ODC?

OD consultancy is seen by some as more appropriate for more mature organisations as *'ODC needs a level of organisational sophistication'*. More mature NGOs may be more able to see the need for such support as well as be able to manage an intervention effectively (e.g. the relationship with external resource people, selection, writing ToRs). There is a very real danger that a weak NGO will relinquish responsibility. One of the assumptions underlying becoming a learning organisation is that there is an openness and a mature self-confidence in combination with a certain level of security (EASUN 1996a). For more immature organisations ODC is not seen by some as appropriate. They argue that in the early stages of an NGO, capacity-building should be about appropriate resource provision as many are not mature enough even to recognise their need for change.

Certainly the more established NGOs in the case studies benefited in some ways from their maturity, though the smaller, newer NGOs also needed and requested OD interventions. Every organisation *'must know who you are and why you are doing what you are doing to be effective'*. Emergent NGOs have a desperate need to be clear about their vision and so OD has to start from the word go. One consultant stated bluntly that *'it is nonsense that OD is only for established organisations'* and another that *'OD is needed for very small organisations, regardless of age or size'*. If OD is an intervention to make an organisation more adaptive and learning then it will apply across the board though *'for new organisations it may be more about defining identity and strategy while for older ones identifying what they are holding onto from the past'.*

Not only do some of the more emergent NGOs need OD consultancy support, but they may be more open to it. Younger organisations such as TUBA may be more flexible in the early stages of their development having not picked up too much bureaucratic baggage and leaving it open to change. It was also recognised that the larger NGOs are more complex and sometimes more resistant to change than newer, more flexible ones. With larger organisations there are also more logistical constraints such as with one of the cases where *'70 people was too big for the process ... representatives were selected ... but feedback to them did not really work'.* Furthermore OD is not seen as a particularly easy approach in a large established NGO where reduction of staff is needed. In fact it was seen as very damaging that OD was sometimes being equated with redundancies in the context of a changing environment which 'necessitates this'.

Did the Type of Organisation Matter?

According to the cases the type of organisation (e.g. membership or intermediary) did not make OD more or less appropriate, but it did have an influence on the speed and impact of the work. The ABA and Sende cases clearly showed that OD consultancy processes with geographically dispersed, voluntaristic, membership organisations necessarily take much longer. Furthermore, the power dynamics of such membership organisations also make them more difficult to change. OD is needed by NGOs of all types, though the impact of ODC (and any other capacity-building interventions for that matter) will vary depending on its nature.

What is Different about OD and Churches?
OD and Churches[1]

Church-related development agencies are becoming increasingly interested in whether OD can have any impact on strengthening the effectiveness of churches in implementing development work.

Churches[2] in Africa have been increasingly receiving outside funding for implementing development programmes for a number of reasons including:

- their having a number of comparative advantages over many 'normal' NGOs because they are a much more rooted part of civil society and therefore have greater legitimacy. They have usually been there longer; will be there 'for

---

[1] Largely derived from the work of Liz Goold at INTRAC.
[2] The term church is used loosely to cover the wide variety of Christian denominations. While they are extremely heterogeneous in nature and form, many of these common characteristics apply.

ever'; are more indigenous (despite some of their missionary roots); have a strong value base (concern for the poor); have a culture of giving; hold regular membership meetings; have a broad village-based presence even in hostile or remote rural areas; and are part of a wider institutional structure with extensive external linkages.

- the establishment of many church-related development agencies during the 1960s and 1970s in Europe and North America who were anxious to support and fund church-related development programmes in the South. These agencies have been able to access funds, both from the general public (and congregations) and increasingly from official sources such as governments and the European Union.

These Northern church agencies, however, have not been immune from the recent contraction of aid budgets and have been forced to look hard at the development programmes they support in the South. The increasing interest of official donors in the impact of their money has further encouraged this process.

To develop ODC practice which incorporates the particular contexts and cultures of churches, it is necessary to explore some of the particular organisational characteristics which may constrain their developmental effectiveness.

Many churches tend to suffer from issues such as:

Identity

There is a lack of clarity around issues of core purpose and identity. The 'mission' of the church is subject to a wide variety of theological and personal interpretations – is it only about saving souls or reaching out to the whole person (integral/holistic development), or establishing the Kingdom of God here on earth? Most churches have a very eclectic membership and include people with a wide range of understanding.

Dualism

The influence of dualism (the separation of the material and the spiritual) has tended to

STRUCTURAL SEPARATION WITHIN CHURCHES BETWEEN DEVELOPMENT DEPARTMENTS AND PASTORAL MINISTRIES HAVE UNDERMINED OVERALL CLARITY OF VISION AND PURPOSE

129

undermine any attempts to gain greater clarity. Northern church-related NGOs have accessed official funding for development work by their partners in the South with the promise to their back donors that no money would go to 'spiritual' work.

It has meant structural separation within churches between the development department and the pastoral department; as well as in roles. Furthermore, the funding imbalance has created a large divide between the 'professional' paid development staff (with their four-wheel drive vehicles) and the practically voluntary pastoral workers (on foot) as well as removed responsibility from the churches for themselves contributing to development efforts.

Strategy

Closely related to the identity issue is the lack of strategy for meeting the needs of the poor. Jesus said, 'Give to the poor' but without detailing how. Churches have tended to take the easier option of paternalistic giving rather than undertake any rigorous social analysis and work out their underlying theory of development. This is reinforced by commands to love and sacrifice for others which makes it very difficult for churches to say 'No' to meeting very real needs or enforce difficult decisions in programmes and organisation. The frequent absence of a clear model of development underpinned by Christian values exacerbates these strategic weaknesses.

The fact that more material aspects of development are only a part of the overall work of the church has strategic implications when dealing with issues of having to prioritise resource allocation.

'CHURCHES OFTEN OPT FOR PATERNALISTIC APPROACHES TO POVERTY'

Hierarchical Structure

Many churches are characterised by a hierarchical structural nature. Power and authority are invested in bishops, clergy and pastors. Church leaders can be extremely powerful people within their institutions which often clashes with participatory development processes. It can also lead to a culture of passivity within the congregations.

The institutional nature of the church, while being a strength, can also often make them very cumbersome, bureaucratic and unwieldy to work with. Their long histories can sometimes make them very impervious to change.

Staffing
In terms of staffing, religious affiliation can often be more important than the required experience and skills to do the job. Relatively low salaries make 'most pastures greener' and staff turnover becomes an issue. Priests may be given responsibility for development programmes on top of existing duties but with little understanding or concept of how they should be managed.

Beneficiaries
The debate about who should be the beneficiaries of the church development programmes – church members and others – means that in this capacity the church is both operating as an NGO (meeting the needs of others) and a CBO (meeting the needs of its members). This causes organisational dilemmas.

Isolationist Culture
Finally, churches have sometimes been competitive between denominations and isolationist from the NGO sector which has militated against cooperation and learning.

Were there any Major Differences in the OD Processes with Church Organisations Compared to Secular Ones?
The particular example of an OD process with the Diocese of Sende shows that in one sense there is very little difference between OD consultancy with churches and with secular NGOs. The OD process was seen by Sende as *'very very appropriate for church bodies. In fact we all need OD, the reality is that funds are becoming scarcer and that only the strong will survive in the new environment'*. At the end of the day you are still dealing with individuals and vested interests.

While in one sense, some of the inherent organisational issues of churches stand in the way of OD being effective, on the other they show the real need for OD with churches. As with all NGOs (and even development in general) the more needy they are for OD the more obstacles there will be to it being effective. For example, the churches dual role in addressing both spiritual and material needs not only is a key OD issue to deal with, but at the same time makes OD processes *'slower because of needing to get the rest of the organisation committed as well as the development office being involved with other pastoral work'*.

The Sende case revealed a number of general learnings (understanding and relating to the whole picture; commitment and involvement of key stakeholders to process and outcomes; working with a group with enough power, ability, and commitment by the organisation to manage the change process; establishing a sense of urgency; identifying stakeholders and gate-keepers; managing the power points must have political perspective) which in fact hold true for all OD interventions. Yet what is also clear is that the success of this inter-vention is due to a specific understanding of the distinctive characteristics and cul-ture of the church; an appreciation of the theological debates; and an empathy from the consultants. Other interventions spon-sored by the same donor in different parts of Africa, *'did not lead to clear results ... because the local consultants had a limited understanding of church development structures'.*

OD interventions with churches not only need an understanding of the church structures, but can also benefit from the use of 'local metaphors or symbols, which may include appropriate language, folklore, ideology, or in the case of a religious organisation, a theological basis' (Kisare 1996:12). OD consultancy itself, for example, can be seen as very much a part of biblical history. When Moses was leading the Israelites to the Promised Land, Jethro came to him with some very sound organisational advice, 'Listen, Moses. You have too many people reporting to you. We're never going to get to the promised land if you do not delegate some power' (paraphrased in Bridges 1995:39).

This exodus story can also be used to illustrate the nature and tensions inher-ent in organisational change. It clearly shows the importance of leaving behind the ways from Egypt, of 'dying to' old attitudes, outlooks, values, mind-sets, self-images in the Wilderness, before being able to realise the vision of inhab-iting a 'land of milk and honey'. The difficulties, uncertainties and resistance to any 'organisational change', as well as the need for inspired leadership are also obvious from the story.

The need for 'servant leadership', is another increasingly fashionable phrase in business circles, and is well demonstrated by Jesus washing his disciples feet. The body of Christ illustration is a good analogy for the 'systems'

'OD CONSULTANCY CAN BE SEEN AS PART OF BIBLICAL HISTORY?

approach. Many other principles of 'management excellence' and effective OD consultancy can be found in the bible and other religious writings. Allan Kaplan of CDRA states, 'for me the most important thing of all is that an OD practitioner works with love. If there is no love, then more harm can be done than good' (1995: 4) ... resounding echoes of 1 Corinthians 13!

Some African consultants, such as Kisare, argue that potentially conflictive issues such as gender can be better approached by using biblical examples rather than donor conditionalities. 'If, for instance, the Church claims the values of justice and "Good News" to all, then the theme of inclusiveness obviously suggests that gender equity cannot be a foreign issue for the Church' (1996: 12).

As with any OD process, an OD intervention with a church-related development organisation needs to understand the particular context and issues which that organisation faces. It also must seek to adapt the intervention to this church context, not only to overcome some of the particular constraints of this context, but to use some of the culturally appropriate methods for promoting change which already exist within churches.

The Context

The case studies did serve to rebut one of the common preconceptions of some European donors that OD is not appropriate to immature NGO sectors. The evidence (albeit limited) of the case studies from Eritrea, Tanzania and Malawi contradict this position and assert that a young NGO sector needs OD consultancy support as much as more mature NGO sectors (such as exist in South Africa or Kenya), and can benefit from such support too, provided it is appropriately contextualised.

In what Contexts was OD Consultancy an Appropriate Approach?

The wider context in which the NGO operates has a very considerable and often underrated influence on both the need for OD and the impact of an OD consultancy process. As Bebbington and Mitlin point out, 'NGOs and capacity-building are highly vulnerable to the general context in which they are working' (1996: 25). We saw in the previous chapter that it was often changes in the wider environment, such as political change in South Africa or Namibia or donor changes in Europe which were the triggers and external pressures which forced NGOs to adapt to this new reality. OD is often about helping NGOs adjust to a changed external environment.

At the same time, the environment also affects whether OD consultancy (or any other capacity-building method for that matter) is an appropriate, effective, 'fundable' intervention. The case studies showed that the political, social and economic contexts had a major impact on the OD consultancies. In South

Africa, for example, the end of apartheid created a massive need for NGOs to radically rethink their whole identity and role in development (and therefore undertake OD processes). This need was accentuated by many NGOs having traditional funding relationships threatened and in some cases broken. At the same time, the desire to contribute to the 'new South Africa' meant that donors were much more open to funding OD processes than in other countries. In addition, OD in South Africa benefited from a history of questioning, and a desire for change. One client also described how *'the changes in South Africa made us more self-assured of our existence and relevance than before. It made us more free, reflective and self-critical'*. South Africa had the other advantages of a high education level and a ready supply of OD consultants – many of whom might be described as white liberals who did not think it was right to run NGOs themselves, but who wanted to contribute to these NGOs being effective.

Similarly, in Eritrea the recent political climate was conducive to OD. With 'independence', all institutions were questioning how they could contribute most effectively to the new society. The EWDFA had the added advantage in their OD process of being supported by the government and society at large. This translated into significant financial support which freed EWDFA from having to respond to donor demands.

The dual influences of the environment on the need for OD and the impact of an OD intervention are often, however, cross-cutting with the context creating a considerable need, but at the same time constraining the implementation of OD. For example, the NRDN case from Namibia showed that years of poor education for black Namibians made the need for OD with NRDN much greater, but at the same time it meant that *'the OD process will take longer and be more expensive'*. With the Sende and the ABA cases too, it was clear that environmental factors such as the level of literacy and the topography, climate and road systems in the region all served to slow down the OD process and would have slowed down any other capacity-building intervention.

What OD Strategy is Appropriate in Situations of Conflict?

In the context of escalating conflict in many parts of the developing world this is a common question of donors. The potential damage which might be caused by poorly managed OD processes is obvious. There is the danger that in chaotic or war-related situations OD consultancy interventions may not be able to open up important but sensitive topics and if they are able they might surface latent conflict in destructive ways. Certainly donors and OD consultants need to be aware of the limitations in situations where hostility, fear, violence and a lack of accountability abound, where one wrong word may lead to execution. Yet they also need to recognise that 'conflict' is not a homogenous entity – there are many different natures, levels and degrees.

While none of the cases dealt directly with an OD intervention in a situation of external conflict, the OD consultants interviewed had worked in such situations. One of them working with the SRRA in Southern Sudan said *'a country is never always at war. People still need to get on with their lives and do certain activities and dream – working out how they can contribute to peace-building. Enabling that to happen is still OD'*. But there are many more road-blocks and obstacles to effective impact of the process such as a bomb which postponed one of the OD workshops with SRRA or workshop participants continually being rotated to fight at the front. The OD process with SRRA avoided some of the problems of exacerbating conflict as the intervention dealt with just one side in the conflict, united not divided by war. As with the other contextual examples described, the context of conflict does not necessarily make OD consultancy inappropriate, though it has to be adapted and treated with great care, though it may slow down the process (and its impact).

Chapter 6

Key Issues Arising for OD with NGOs

INTRODUCTION

The research highlighted a number of key issues arising for OD consultancy with NGOs some of which had been raised as questions by Northern NGOs at the start of the research. They include questions such as:

- *How can we measure the impact of ODC?*
- *Is OD a cross-cultural imposition?*
- *How does gender and diversity fit with ODC?*
- *Is ODC with churches any different?*
- *What are the main dangers of ODC?*
- *When is ODC not appropriate?*

These issues will be addressed in turn.

EVALUATING OD

How can We Measure the Impact of OD?

One the major concerns of Northern NGOs (and main questions asked of this research) is whether all this investment of time and money in organisational consultancy as opposed to funding projects is a cost-effective use of increasingly limited resources. Southern providers are realising that, 'those who are funding capacity-building now are likely to be asking tough questions about how OD has made things better in the future. Do we have the rigour to monitor and evaluate change over a period of time?' (CDRA 1995:31).

While increasingly desiring this information, European NGOs admit that *'past evaluations have been rather sloppy. Now we include organisational change in original proposal and evaluations'*. In another agency it was stated that *'the process is not very measured or written down'* and yet another respondent said, *'I don't know yet (how successful OD is) – we just do it so far. In theory we sit with the organisations and discuss what has changed ...'.* The poor quality of the information regarding the effectiveness of OD can be linked to the inherent methodological and practical problems in measurement.

'Does it work?' is the simplest of questions, but is very difficult to answer definitively and comprehensively. It is much easier to answer the question, 'can it work?' but again hard to determine always 'why does it work?' and identify relevant causal mechanisms. There are both inherent methodological and practical issues to confront.

Methodological Problems with the Evaluation of OD
1. Definitional
What is an OD consultancy?
OD is not a precise term and is subject to endless variations, interpretations and intervention methodologies (which may themselves change over time). How much of an ongoing process does it have to be to be called OD? How much of an organisation must it deal with? How many of the phases of the consultancy process must be carried through to be called OD? Can poorly implemented OD, which contravenes the norms of good practice, still be called OD? Since 'OD is not precisely defined; not reducible to specific, uniform, observable behaviours' (Khan 1974 quoted in Burke 1987:134) evaluation of such a slippery concept is difficult.

What exactly is meant by 'effective'?
Furthermore, there are considerable problems also in defining what is greater organisational effectiveness (the goal of OD). Not only are there a number of different models of effectiveness such as the goal model, system resource model, process model or strategic constituencies model but very different understandings of development. As one respondent put it, 'poverty is such a complex and terrifying creature – what return are you looking for, is it human capital; political; economic at a household or local level?'

Effective from whose perspective?
Even if these are defined the very real questions (in all evaluation) remain, 'who defined it and how'. At times different stakeholders (and different staff members) may have very different perspectives on the same intervention. It is difficult to differentiate an individual perspective from an organisational one, especially if many people naturally object to change (even if it is good for them).

2. The Problem of Attribution
'Success has many parents ... failure is an orphan.' African Proverb (Newens

ORGANISATIONS ARE VERY NOISY
ENVIRONMENTS.....

and Roche 1996:7)

Even if you are sure that an organisation is performing better after an OD intervention, it is very difficult to prove a direct causal link between the intervention and the greater effectiveness. In organisations so much is ongoing you cannot isolate single factors as an independent variable if other variables cannot be easily controlled. It is said that, *'organisations are very noisy environments. That is at any given time many changes, planned and unplanned may be taking place'* (Walters 1990:219).

To make matters more complicated, consultancy (as opposed to hands-on implementation) is a limited intervention which exacerbates the problem of attribution. Long-term change is out of the hands of the OD consultant as it relies on the organisation itself. However perfect an intervention, it can be undermined if the organisation does not implement change itself for reasons outside the consultant's control. To overcome this inherent problem of attribution, you need a highly controlled experimental approach which is not usually a cost-effective option.

3. The Counter-Factual

Closely linked to the problem of attribution is the issue of the 'counter-factual' – how have changes in the overall context affected the effectiveness of the intervention. As one respondent put it, *'you can spend years building the capacity of an organisation, when something happens in the wider system which has an overwhelming impact and undermines the effect of the change process'*. It might be factors such as recession, war, natural disasters, funding cuts or even internal issues unrelated to the consultancy. In such cases, it might be possible that although on the surface it appears that the intervention has done little, if it had not taken place the situation may have been much worse.

As with any evaluation the starting base needed to be taken into account of any attempt to measure effectiveness is *'the more marginalised the people are that you are dealing with (without education) the more you will have to invest to get a similar return'*.

4. Problems of Instrumentation, Access and Research Bias

The need for control or experimental groups is very difficult in OD field research. Just as with this research, organisations involved in OD self-select themselves making random assignment almost impossible. Furthermore, there are very real issues about who will conduct the research and how 'external' they can be. Too close involvement with OD can lead to suggestions of consultant bias, too distant involvement raises very real problems of access.

Practical Problems with the Evaluation of OD

As well as these methodological issues in an evaluation of OD there are very real practical issues to grapple with:

Lack of Time and Money

In the action-oriented NGO culture, there is rarely sufficient time and money set aside for evaluation. As NGO resources become scarcer, it is likely that, although donors will demand more evidence of impact, there will be even less resources available for evaluating capacity-building initiatives. Questions were raised in the research as to whether such attempts to empirically measure effectiveness were even worthwhile. One African respondent was 'not sure the process of trying to establish cost-effectiveness would be itself cost-effective'.

Long-Term Nature of Results

Respondents from both Africa and Europe pointed to the fact that the results of any OD intervention are very long term, saying that if you really want to measure impact 'come back in ten years time to evaluate'. If capacity-building is the long-term process which organisations like USAID and DFID admit it is (USAID 1989), and as most European NGO experience of OD is limited to just two years, then it is not surprising that NGOs believe that it is too early to arrive at considered conclusions about the effectiveness of OD yet, however much they would like to.

Evaluation Attempts may even be Counter-Productive

Southern respondents were concerned that *'as soon as you bring in questions of cost effectiveness you force a compromise on quality'* because as Tandon states 'hooking capacity-building to measurable targets of organisational performance can result in short-term pumping of the existing priorities as opposed to long-term positioning of strategic requirements' (1997a).

Donor Role in the Process

The task of evaluation is made doubly difficult for Northern NGOs by their donor role in the process. Ideally, as it is the Southern NGO which is the client, the Northern NGO is not part of the feedback loop. According to one European NGO, *'this means that if interventions are mediocre we never know. It has to be very bad to hear a negative report'*.

Yet there is a Need for Evaluation

Despite these constraints and obstacles, an evaluation of OD consultancy approaches to capacity-building is necessary for clients, consultants and funders. As NGOs in a changed funding environment, we need to be much more concerned with issues of impact. In the inimitable words of one official agency, *'if you cannot measure it, you cannot manage it'*. If NGOs do not attempt some form of evaluation themselves, it will be imposed on them from outside. Although there are dangers in evaluation, there are also many potential benefits. It forces a definition of objectives, outcomes and indicators which encourages specificity, and signals problems and obstacles which need to be tackled.

As with all monitoring and evaluation, different stakeholders have different perceptions. Seeing consultancy as a network of relationships means that analysis of its effectiveness must be holistic to take account of the contribution made by different individuals and organisations involved (Arthur and Preston 1996). INTRAC firmly believes in a more 'interpretive' approach to evaluation where a multiplicity of stakeholder perceptions are sought and where some attempt is made to grasp measures of performance.

How to Evaluate

The success of an OD intervention can be measured against the objectives of the OD intervention. This can best be done when the objectives and indicators of success are developed by the client NGO at the start of the organisational change process. These objectives should be outlined during the contracting stage when the terms of reference are drawn up. They can be further developed during the diagnosis stage (often a joint analysis workshop is useful for this as key stakeholders themselves identify the major changes necessary and how such changes might be measured). In the long term it can be seen whether the stated areas of change were reached.

What to Evaluate
There are three main areas which can be evaluated:

1. internal organisational changes;
2. external changes in the beneficiary group or NGO external relations;
3. the OD process itself.

1. Internal Organisational Changes
One of the major triggers for an OD intervention is that it is facing some sort of crisis and that unless it changes things are going to get much worse - sometimes even the very organisation's existence is threatened. For a realistic assessment of the impact of an OD intervention, the situation after the end of the intervention should be compared with the actual situation beforehand as well as with predictions of what would have happened without the intervention. For example, for the NGO to have survived at all may be a major indictor of impact.

One of the major goals of OD, which was identified in the definition of OD is to ensure that the client develops the capacity to take on its own change processes in the future. There should be evidence that the organisational change process is ongoing and that the client demonstrates the ability to solve its own problems.

There has been significant work done in the last few years developing organisational assessment tools which identify key organisational indictors (INTRAC has collected over 50 such tools). These include indictors relating to the organisation's:

- learning, openness and ability to manage change;
- identity (e.g. being assertive with donors and able to turn down funding);
- governance (having a board which is involved and committed to making the NGO effective);
- mission (having a purpose which is clear, understood and shared);
- strategy (having clear strategies which guide decisions on activities);
- systems (having established systems for decision-making, communication, monitoring and evaluation, personnel, administrative, financial etc.);
- structures (having a structure which made sense in relation to the NGO's mission and strategy);
- staffing (having competent and committed staff);
- internal relationships and morale (the staff and management working together coherently and positively);
- financial and physical resources (having adequate resources in both the short and long terms to reach the programme objectives).

These indicators need to take into account the different capacities required by NGOs at different stages of their development.

2. External Changes
It is clear that capacity-building of NGOs is not an end in itself, but a means to improving the well-being of poor people. Donors are concerned that changes resulting from OD interventions remain at the organisational level and are never translated into changes at the level of beneficiaries. It is important therefore that rigorous evaluation of OD processes should elicit the views of the ultimate beneficiaries, though access to them may be difficult for outsiders.

While the goal of an OD intervention is to improve the performance of that organisation, it may be that in the longer term other organisations are indirectly, but significantly, affected too. For example, the OD process may well have significant impacts on individuals which are not able to be translated into organisational changes until they leave and join other organisations.

3. Evaluating the OD Process Itself
One of the more straightforward ways of evaluating an OD consultancy intervention is to concentrate on evaluating the process itself. In many ways this is fairer on the consultant as s/he is able to control the intervention process to a large degree, whereas the internal or external changes are much more in the hands of the client. According to EASUN, where the responsibility to implement change lies so much with the client organisation itself, 'the success of OD can mainly be assessed in good consultancy practice' (Annual Report 1995/6 :7). Significant events such as survey-feedback workshops, training, conflict resolution meetings can be evaluated by participants, as well as other factors such as the client consultant relationship; and the project consultant's time and expense budgets against actual.

If the balance of evidence in these areas, from the perceptions of different stakeholders in the process (particularly from the beneficiaries), is positive then we can get a useful sense of the success of the intervention. According to Riddell, 'it is unnecessary to concentrate time, effort and resources on evaluation if firm conclusions can be drawn without using sophisticated techniques. Similarly if judgements made about the qualitative aspects of projects are not substantially challenged by the relevant actors or groups ... then purist worries about objectively assessing these factors become largely irrelevant' (quoted in Newens and Roche 1996:7).

CULTURE AND OD

Is OD a Cross-Cultural Imposition in Africa?

One of the major criticisms which OD faces in Africa comes largely from Western academics who claim that not only is OD a foreign approach to managing change, but that it is not cross-culturally transferable. Some remark on

> the absurdity of technique peddling by Western management consultants in Africa, exemplified by bizarre attempts to undertake organisation development (OD) consultancies (with their accompanying American individualistic, humanistic values) in African organisations. (Hyden quoted in Jones and Mann 1983:110)

Certainly one prime factor influencing the effectiveness of OD work is the cultural context in which the organisation is located. Moreover, because the OD process evolved largely from experience with commercial firms in the United States, OD values and accompanying assumptions (examined in Chapter 1) about openness, collaboration and expression of feelings may not fit many non-Western cultures. One of the main writers in this field, Kalburgi Srinivas asserts that

> the dominant current thinking of OD practitioners is that this cultural receptivity factor has worked against the utilisation of OD interventions in developing countries ... Many of the efforts to apply OD approach and associated techniques to the developing world have raised doubts that perhaps the field of OD as it has emerged to date is culture specific, that it may simply not travel well to locations outside its birth-place. (Srinivas 1993:18)

Cultural Clash?

Much of the work on the cross-cultural transferability of OD has used Hofstede's dimensions of culture. Developing countries[1] are seen as more distant to OD values because they 'are characterised by high power distance and high uncertainty avoidance. Clearly these values are strongly opposed to many of those underlying process consulting' (Blunt 1995:11).

High power distance

Many OD interventions focus on groups and require face-to-face interaction (confrontation?) across hierarchical levels and yet 'in high power distance societies for example it is unlikely that it would be possible to achieve frank and open communication between members of different hierarchical levels operating in the same problem-solving group. Participation by junior members is likely to be more symbolic than real' (Blunt 1995:10). Moreover, Hofstede proposes that subordinates in high power distance settings have strong dependence needs and expect superiors to behave autocratically and not to consult them – they are likely to feel uncomfortable if they do.

Uncertainty avoidance

It is said that many developing countries are also characterised by wanting to avoid situations of uncertainty implying that staff are 'unlikely to want to engage in activities which are unstructured or whose outcomes are unpre-

---

[1] It is very dangerous to make sweeping generalisations about inherently dynamic national cultures, let alone continental cultures – there are usually significant regional or ethnic differences which make the situation much more complex.

dictable, particularly if conflict or aggression is likely to be involved. People in such cultures have high needs for security and expect their leaders to be assertive' (Blunt 1995:11).

In a more specific study of OD transferability in Latin America, Bourgeois and Boltvinik (1981) noted that there were inherent conflicts between OD and Latin American cultures. There was a rejection of OD power equalisation principles while authoritarian management styles are not only accepted but practically demanded by both workers and subordinate managers. They concluded that this maintenance of pronounced hierarchic formality and social distance presents a considerable barrier to the informality and intimacy sought in some OD programmes.

Some writers on OD in Africa have pointed to similar constraints 'African culture discourages innovativeness, individualism, or impersonalism and anything that prevents or challenges the valued social order and stability' (Chowdhury 1986 quoted in Blunt 1995) or 'traditional African cultures embody a respect for the person as part of society and value social interaction and interdependence as central to life in the community. There is a less critical attitude to individual performance and a high respect for age and experience' (Srinivas 1995:207).

As a result Blunt and Jones conclude that 'there must be considerable doubt concerning the ability of African organisations to initiate and manage change' (1992:231).

Others even question whether African cultures would have the goal of improving organisational performance: 'the desirability of improving organisational performance, which is a central value in the West may be secondary to social and political objectives' (ODA report quoted by Blunt 1995:19). African organisations are seen by some as social constructs, concerned with developing relationships and establishing authority rather than following the Western instrumental view of organisations being set up for task achievement.

Some limitations of this perspective

While it is clear that there are clearly some extremely important cross-cultural issues which must be taken into account to avoid the 'bizarre attempts' to impose OD in another culture, it seems that much of the criticism of OD in developing countries comes from writers who:

- use a 'romantic primitivism' caricature of African culture rather than seeing African cultures as very heterogeneous – a dynamic and eclectic mix of a number of influences including the traditional, the Western and the Eastern. The changing nature of many African cultures can be seen in the significant differences between rural and urban areas even within the same ethnic group.

- use a limited, outdated and oversimplified definition of OD as merely group process interventions. The theory and practice of OD has moved considerably since its almost exclusive focus on group processes in the 1960s and 1970s. It has recently become much more concerned with macro and strategic issues which have a more immediate link with performance.

- fail to distinguish between poor implementation of OD and the nature of OD *per se*.

Much of the OD that has been carried out so far in developing countries has been done by expatriates. The current aid system means many OD projects are sponsored by international agencies and foreign aid agencies of developing nations and as a result that 'there is still a rush to use expatriates' (Bassuyt, Laporte and van Hoek 1992:3 quoted in Arthur and Preston 1996:16), but as Kiggundu concluded from his ILO study in Asia and Africa, it does matter whether the change agent is a foreigner or a local national as the degree of change agent awareness and understanding of the local culture often determines the fate of an intervention. As Srinivas notes, 'the change agents are outsider to the culture and change models are exogenous, thus minimising the possibilities of real change' (1995:217). The aid system exacerbates these issues as foreign change agents are not given the time, incentive or mandate to develop appropriate cultural understanding. The current preference for short-term consultancies is not conducive to the effective transfer of OD.

Furthermore, some foreign consultants have failed to live up to professional and ethical standards even within their own cultural norms: 'foreign consultants have failed to prove themselves, enforced by donors for their own interests ... they are arrogant, overbearing, with lifestyles which take no account of their surroundings' (Kariuki J in Kaijage 1993:24). It should be noted, however, that local consultants may have similar problems and be just as out of touch with the rural poor, while facing additional problems because 'African managers unsure of their own competence are not so keen to expose their shortcomings to outsiders particularly other Africans asking: "what can I learn from another African, after all I went to the same school"' (Kariuki J in Kaijage 1993:28).

So much of the rejection of ODC is from where it is done badly by culturally insensitive consultants. These consultants may have pushed too much in using techniques which aim to increase group collaboration and cooperation which do stir emotions, values and hidden matters. In many countries expressing feelings in public forums is inappropriate and so interventions at deep levels need to heed cultural sensitivities. The rule of thumb is that a consultant should proceed no faster or deeper than the legitimation obtained from the client system and that s/he stays at the level of consciously felt needs (Srinivas 1995) with occasional but prudent pushing, rather than quantum jumps (French and Bell 1984). The question is not so much does OD travel well, but do the OD consultants themselves travel well? Experience is showing that it is more a question of the personal values, approaches, sensitivities and behaviours of individuals and how they practice OD, rather than anything inherent in OD itself.

So it may not be OD which is so culturally bound, but poor practice of OD. The same could be said of most interventions. Bad practice is rarely cross-culturally transferable.

'OD Concurs with African Cultures Too'

Many African practitioners (in contrast to Western academics) argue that in fact there are many elements of African culture which actually promote and re-inforce the use of OD rather than undermine it. They claim that from being cross-culturally untransferrable, OD consultancy builds on many African cultural norms because 'traditional African approaches to managing change are: collective ceremonies and rituals, story tellers, dancing and music as well as facilitation by an outside soothsayer and sangoma' (Mbigi 1995:110).

African ways of managing change in communities are often through working with the whole organisation or community. For training to move from collective talk to collective action it needs to harness the collective energy and support of key players. According to Mbigi 'one needs to use open collective forums which are inclusive in nature and must as much as possible include everyone in the organisation' (1995:111). Such open collective forums are common in African culture. Mbigi describes 'pungwes' as open forums, all night renewal ceremonies which focus on issues of survival and yet allow space for the community to explore gut issues. Such descriptions of 'pungwes' seem very akin to the frequent OD practice of facilitating a participative workshop for the organisation to explore key problem areas.

Another traditional element of managing change in Africa is using an outside mediator or soothsayer to encourage the process: 'you cannot change culture from within. In African culture you are not encouraged to change the habits of your spouse. This role is always played by a mediator. They constantly come in and hear the unspoken grievances and to say the unsayable' (Mbigi 1995:112). Furthermore the 'open forums must be led by an outside facilitator' which make the role of an outside OD consultant very familiar. In Malawi there is a Chichewa proverb which says, 'it is the stranger who brings the sharper blade'.

Does African OD Exist?

The African practitioners interviewed during the research would certainly take the view that OD is appropriate in Africa. They argue, *'what is foreign about the OD process I have described?'* another stating, *'the principles of OD are not foreign'* and another client describing the OD process as *'a true African approach'*. ESAMI[2] would also assert that OD is effective in Africa, stating that, 'in (our) judgement, which is based on the experience in at least 7 counties in Africa, process consultancy is the most effective approach in sub-Saharan Africa' ... 'The best and tested method for building the capacity of institutions is the process consultancy approach' (Mbise and Shirima in Kaijage 1993: 143).

There was recognition that there are cultural differences about participative decision-making processes and confrontation, for example, which might appear to make OD difficult to implement, but that given an understanding of the culturally appropriate way these processes do occur in Africa, possible contradictions (if they did exist) would be minimised. Certainly there may be less eyeball-to-eyeball confrontation in Africa, but for example *'if you have a disagreement with your father, you will go and talk to your mother who will go and talk to your father'*. The confrontation of problems does exist, though the mechanisms are different. Similarly democratic decision-making processes are there if not immediately apparent to the outsider. Nelson Mandela describes the profound influence of the decision-making processes of the Thembu people of which his grandfather was chief,

> everyone who wanted to speak could do so. It was democracy in its purest sense. There may have been a hierarchy importance amongst the speakers, but everyone was heard ... Only at the end of the meeting as the sun was setting would the regent speak. His purpose was to sum up what had been said and form some consensus among the diverse opinions. But no conclusion was forced on those who disagreed. (Mandela 1994:20)

At the same time as minimising some of the more obvious differences between traditional African cultures and OD processes, there was also the recognition that African culture is not only very heterogeneous (with some tribes very change resistant for example), but also very dynamic. In some cases cultures are becoming more directly open to such OD processes. For instance, it was mentioned that some of constraining African ways are changing, such as more participative decision-making. One OD consultant commented, *'we have rejected what was and are clamouring for what should be. We have lost many of our tra-*

---

[2] Eastern and Southern African Management Institute.

ditional ways and are better at knowing Western ideas than our own'. If OD does conflict, it is less so than before.

It is more often the techniques and methods used by OD consultants which are foreign, not the values and principles underlying it, *'you can just as easily use African models, tools, proverbs'* rather than confrontational T-groups for example. Such adaptation can take place on a variety of levels from the very simple level of stories and proverbs and even pictures. For example, the traditional OD image of culture as an iceberg may not be too relevant in Africa – the hippo we saw in Chapter 1 might be a more familiar and dynamic example.

Rather than using foreign concepts, local proverbs or local folk-tales can be used. For example in Malawi discussions of organisational change have used the proverb, *'if you want to change someone you must start at the heart'* (Mukafuna kusintha munthu, muyambe m'mtima) or when looking at strategic planning: *'here delicious things, there delicious things, the monkey ends up falling flat on his back'* (Ichi chakoma, ichi chakoma pusi anagwa chagada) or *'bad things do not beat a drum to say they are coming so be prepared'* (Chakudza sichiimba n'goma) or for team-building, *'one finger does not squash a tick'* (Chala chimodzi sichiswa nsabwe).

Another example from Mbigi shows the extent of integration:

> The General Manager and I would go over the company's strategic objectives and each pause would be punctuated by songs and slogans, designed to capture the company's vision. Cattle were slaughtered. There would be a lot of singing, tribal dancing and eating. The ceremony represented a synthesis of Western values and South African visionary spirit. (Mbigi in Christie et al. 1993:82)

OD does have to be modified to fit the local culture as 'OD practices that do not deliberately weave in the cultural heritage may not have a chance to affect deeper levels' (Srinivas 1995:218). 'Foreign' OD concepts and techniques should not be blindly rejected in Africa, but rather should be applied with careful alterations based on indigenous values and ideas of development. A contingency approach to organisational change is needed.

This need for cultural adaptation should not be underestimated and 'prior to cross-cultural OD intervention, extensive research should be done within the culture, to ascertain what values, preferences and inclinations exist there that would bear on the choice or development of OD technology' (Bourgeois and Boltvinik 1981:79). One aspect which is necessary to take on board is that 'the most pervasive and fundamental collective experience of African people is their religious experience' (Mbigi 1995:2) and yet OD is still largely a humanistic approach to change. Another, as we saw clearly from the cases, is that the OD process in Africa has to go at the pace of the people and adapt both conceptually and linguistically. Geoff Mamputa, a local consultant, describes a visioning process he was conducting with a farmers group in Northern Natal:

> Finally I asked the group, 'where do you see this organisation in 5 years time?' All eyes shifted to an old man in his 80s. 'My son I have been in this world a very long time. These eyes have seen a lot ... but to ask us to see into the future is one of the most difficult things to do. Only God and nezangoma can do that ...' After discussing the old man's statement for 3 hours or so we did reach an agreement that, 'God willing, this is how we would like to see this organisation in 5 years time.' (1997:7)

Such adaptions also require 'a critical understanding of that which is being adapted' (Cooke 1996b:3). It is very rare to find both an organisational expertise and an anthropological perspective combined. One or the other usually predominates. In fact, such adaption will improve and add to OD practice in the West as 'Africa's achievements and genius do not lie in technology, but in social and spiritual fields. Social innovation, the crafting of relevant organisational collective rituals and ceremonies ... has to be brought to the centre of organisational transformation and renewal in Africa' (Mbigi 1995:4) and then disseminated abroad!

The question then changes from 'how can we adapt OD to the local culture?' to 'what aspects of the local culture can be built on to create an African OD?'.

Does OD Fit an NGO Culture?

The practice of OD consultancy is taken largely from the commercial sector, so even an adaption of OD to the African context is not enough. It must also be adapted to the NGO context too. Management solutions are often imported to the NGO sector wholesale without any understanding or experience of the distinct organisational features of NGOs. In the case of OD, however, it may well be that OD is in fact a more appropriate approach to change in the NGO sector than in the public or private sectors due to the fact that both OD and NGOs share values such as participation and empowerment.

OD enjoys a common philosophy and approach with many of the Participative Action Research (PAR) initiatives which are emerging from developing countries and NGO experience. Community-based techniques such as Participatory Rural Appraisal (PRA) have much in common with participative OD techniques. Often the most significant difference is only that PRA initiatives tend to focus the intervention on the community, while OD consultancy tends to focus on the organisation.

The albeit limited experience of OD within the NGO sector certainly seems positive as 'our experience in working very closely with one organisation has shown that this may be a very fruitful approach to the development of a voluntary organisation' (Chattopadhyay and Pareek 1984:83).

GENDER, DIVERSITY AND OD

Are Gender Issues Part of OD?

Gender awareness and gender planning are key NGO capacities which often need to be improved from the perspectives of both justice and efficiency. An organisation must respond properly to the needs of all its clients/members (and in development the majority of poor and marginalised people are women) as well as make full use of the pool of talent available. But gender and diversity issues are often externalised by NGOs as problems out there with programmes. Issues of gender and diversity reach to the very core of an organisation internally too: who holds power; how are decisions made; how communication occurs; what staff terms and conditions exist?

Gender and diversity issues are at the heart of OD and change and yet despite the simultaneous rise of both gender and OD as key issues for NGOs, they have tended to develop in relative isolation from each other. Each discipline appears to have been more concerned with protecting and reinforcing its own identity, rather than opening itself up to and learning from others. As a result approaches to gender and OD have developed in parallel, characterised more by mutual suspicion than integration. Gender practitioners have not used the instruments developed by OD practitioners and gender dynamics of organisations have not often been seen as part of OD interventions. Gender specialists have argued that OD is merely a small part of the whole gender issue and have tended to see organisational problems as being exclusively gender-related, while OD specialists have argued that gender is merely one aspect of OD.

This parallel development has led to situations of duplication where, for example, in one NGO, a consultant was called in to do a gender analysis and another one to do an organisational analysis. Both consultants presented the organisation with different strategies to integrate gender into the organisation's work and to tackle its organisational issues.

Over the past two years, however, there has been increased interest (particularly from the Dutch NGOs Novib and Hivos) to learn how gender and OD can mutually enrich each other. A recent workshop in Harare was designed to do just that by bringing together OD and gender consultants from all over Eastern and Southern Africa. The introduction to the workshop asserted that 'given the transitional stage of many countries, OD and gender are among the key interventions used to manage this process of transition, and for moving systems and people towards change' (Made and Maramba 1997:1).

There is considerable overlap between OD and approaches to gender issues and significant scope for each area reinforcing the other. They both look at people within organisations, both are trying to bring about attitude and behaviour change. They face very similar issues in implementation with NGOs such as that of power within organisations; cross-cultural applicability; the appropriate role of the donor; the required consultancy skills, attitudes, experience; the need for donors to put their own house in order and of course the need for the NGO to have ownership of change.

In fact in many publications dealing with good practice in gender or OD, one could merely substitute the terms and the document would still make sense! Both gender and OD use very similar interventions. The Harare workshop found that 'gender interventions for the most part are not really different from OD interventions. These include strategic planning, management and leadership development, self-understanding, skills training, conflict resolution, team-building, decision making/power dynamics, organisational culture ...' (Made and Maramba 1997:3).

This is not to say that working on gender issues and OD are the same or indistinguishable. There are significant differences as gender is broader than OD in that, for example, gender activism can exist on its own outside any organisational structure context. OD is also broader than just gender (or even issues of diversity) in dealing with issues of identity, mission, strategy, systems, skills and structures. Gender issues certainly impinge on all these areas, but they are not the only influence.

There are, however, significant areas where each should learn from the other. Approaches to gender bring very significant understandings to the OD process which should not be ignored. These include the recognition that all organisations are gendered. Men and women are situated differently within organisational structures (structures tend to be patriarchal and meet men's needs better than those of women's); organisational cultures operate differently for men and women (usually favouring men over women); women's and men's work is valued differently in the organisation. This has an important impact on the NGO's programmes performance and impact with beneficiaries, as Goetz points out 'gendered internal structures and practices actually produce gendered outcomes and personnel who, whatever their sex, reproduce gender discriminatory outcomes' (quoted in Macdonald et al. 1997:26).

The gender perspective also brings the positive recognition that gender-sensitive organisations are more effective in that not only are they better able to respond to the needs of their beneficiaries (most of the poor and marginalised being women), but they are also better able to make full use of the pool of talent available within the organisation. Women in a subordinated position within organisations cannot enrich that organisation and the best ones may soon leave. Improving the gender perspective within NGOs not only can improve their effectiveness, but also deals with a political issue of justice. Most NGOs artic- ulate values of justice for the poor and marginalised. Incorporating gender per- spectives into their organisations and programmes allows them greater coher- ence and consistency between their espoused values and their practised ones.

Organisational approaches to gender can also teach OD through its empha- sis and understanding of power dynamics within NGOs. OD has tended in the past to steer clear of issues of power and there is a general acceptance that OD consultants need to understand them much better and work with them to bring about organisational change. Attempts to bring about positive changes in gen- der in NGOs have grappled with issues of power for many years. Gender spe- cialists have considerable hands-on experience with attempting to bring about organisational change from which OD consultants for NGOs should learn. For example, the only OD intervention written up on BRAC, the largest NGO in the world, deals with a programme to bring about organisational changes in terms of gender.

On the other hand, gender can learn much from the OD discipline. OD brings an understanding of the dynamics and processes of organisational change. According to the UK National Council for Voluntary Organisations the reason why all the efforts and resources poured into equal opportunities up until now have achieved so little is because 'its implementation has rarely been approached as a major change requiring careful and systematic planning and execution' (quoted in May 1994). For gender interventions to be successful and to have a long-term impact they have to be based on insights into organisation- al dynamics, history, culture and the external environment of an organisation. Otherwise gender will not be part of an ongoing process of organisational change and development and therefore not part of the core business or heart of an organisation. OD brings an experience and emphasis of the need for change to often be at a deeper level of organisational culture.

Tactically, OD is being seen by some gender specialists as less threatening than gender interventions. While gender on its own can be threatening, if it is packaged into an OD intervention it can be empowering. Gender is seen as inherently a more emotional and emotive issue because we are all affected directly in one way or another and it is impossible to compartmentalise gender issues into work life. OD consultancy can be used to provide the space to intro- duce gender onto the NGO's agenda, though there is the danger that as a result gender will become hidden (and lost) within OD. OD consultants need to be knowledgeable about the linkages between OD and gender as well as to model them in their attitudes and behaviours.

OD and gender need to be integrated. Gender is a fundamental aspect of organisations; change and power. Gender should always be a part of OD as OD requires a holistic understanding of the organisation, though gender may not always necessarily be the priority issue with which to deal. An organisation's strategy for achieving its purpose may be more critical and even if issues of diversity do need urgent attention, gender is only one (albeit key) aspect of diversity and it may be more important to address issues of race or ethnicity.

What about Diversity and OD?

The last few years have seen the increasing practice of integrating gender concerns into NGO policies and programmes. At the same time, however, the debate seems to have shifted from an exclusive focus on gender to a broader focus on issues of diversity. It is becoming clearer that you cannot simply address issues of gender without exploring other aspects of diversity and difference such as race, ethnicity, geographic origin, disability and age. As well as gender, OD should embrace these wider issues, which interestingly appear to be more culturally appealing to some African NGOs than what some see as the 'European' agenda of gender.

How was Gender Built into the OD Consultancies?

Most of the cases illustrate the traditional separation of gender from OD. From the case studies it does not appear that gender issues were specifically addressed, except in the TUBA strategic directions work, where gender awareness and analysis exercises and methods were successfully integrated into each day of the workshop (and that was mainly at the request of the donor!).

It proved quite difficult to access good case studies where OD and gender were addressed as integrated and important in their own right, even from the European NGOs such as Novib and Hivos who are championing such an approach.

The remaining cases deal with gender more indirectly through:

- a mixed consultancy team;
- consultants and providers having a reputation for gender awareness;
- interventions focusing on a diversity of stakeholders;
- techniques which bring out the views of women, youth and other more marginalised sections.

The OD consultants interviewed during the research were very positive about the role of gender and OD. Some could see a clear relationship, pointing out that *'you can see a very different masculine and feminine culture in organisations which affects the way you should intervene. Masculine is about boundaries, strategic direction, strength out there in the world, while feminine is about sup-*

port, caring. *Feminine organisations tend not to like strategy and often foster dependence. As consultants we need to swim the opposite poles'.* Another thought that *'gender should be a part of OD. Unless you are very conscious, your OD intervention may simply reinforce masculine managerialism and hierarchy'.* Some OD consultants were seen to perpetuate gender stereotypes and used 'right-on' words as mere lip-service to gender.

Others were more ambivalent feeling that *'gender is not a specific part of OD, though if men dominate then that obviously has to be dealt with'.* There was a feeling that gender issues needed cultural interpretation and as such a reaction against a purely European definition of gender. They were also concerned at the danger that gender can become a limiting factor excluding other factors of diversity and certainly the cases dealt more with wider questions of diversity such as colour, race and age.

THE POTENTIAL DANGERS OF ODC

What are the Potential Dangers of ODC?
ODC is vulnerable to many potential dangers and limitations which need to be considered before an OD intervention and borne in mind throughout the process. Such dangers include the following:

Too Much is Expected of ODC
OD consultancy is seen by some to be the new panacea for development and capacity-building of NGOs. Too much is expected of outside interventions which can at best facilitate an organisation in changing. Even if some problems have been successfully dealt with, new problems will emerge as the environment changes or people change. It is unhelpful to be under the false, though often unconscious, assumption that an organisation's problems will be over an OD intervention.

Limitations of Consultancy
Linked to this issue is the fact that many of the limitations of OD are also the inherent limitations of any consultancy. The consultant cannot be responsible for the change process within the organisation. The NGO has to do it itself. For example, a strategic review can make suggestions for the future, but it is up to the organisation to implement. Weisbord describes this as 'we always arrive in the middle of someone else's movie and leave before the end' (1987:13) or as Hanson and Lubin say 'we cannot change other people. We can, however, create conditions that make change less threatening and in which others may chose to change. The responsibility for change lies with the client' (1995:116).

It was clear that if change took place after an OD intervention much depended on the NGO itself, rather than necessarily the quality of the intervention. The TUBA strategic directions process was slowed by the abrupt removal of the director for fraud and the planned departure of three key staff members as well as the chair of the board. The ensuing leadership vacuum further delayed implementation of some of the strategic decisions. The ABA case also revealed that *'while the intervention of EASUN was great implementation since has been poor'*.

One of the consultants clearly expressed the limitations of consultants and consulting saying, *'I have more respect for the innate life processes of organisations to believe that I can engineer change. All I did was help them face up to an unconscious question by putting it firmly on the table'*.

Process Weaknesses

There are also often a number of weaknesses in the way that the OD consultancy process is implemented in practice.

OD Consultancy is Expensive

OD consultancy is an expensive intervention because it is very time-consuming and labour intensive. It also requires experienced and able practitioners who cost more than mere fly-by-night cowboys! This makes many donors see OD as too expensive to implement properly. Arthur and Preston conclude that the cost of OD consultancy 'frequently inhibits donor and broker willingness to endorse consultancy which more than minimally involves members of a host country organisation or end user groups' Arthur and Preston 1996: 30)

There is a need to balance the outcomes of an OD consultancy with the costs and the overall turnover of the organisation. It is also important to factor in the cost to the NGO in terms of time, given that they cannot close down during the OD process, but have to maintain programme activities at the same time. For Northern NGOs, it should be recognised that OD consultancy is time consuming even to manage and only a few such initiatives can be handled at any one time.

OD Consultancy is often Cut Short

The need for a heavy investment of time means there is always the temptation to cut short or truncate the OD process. In an evaluation of one of the main providers of OD services in Southern Africa, more than half the clients were not happy with the extent of the follow-up. This was either because they wanted more interventions or because the intervention started internal conflicts or because they were unable to implement the recommendations. OD is rarely given enough time by the NGO, the consultant or the donor and as a result runs the risk of being used in piecemeal fashion.

OD Process may Go too Far
OD consultancy also runs the risk of being disabling by raising the conscious-ness of an organisation beyond its capacity to act. OD consultancy therefore needs to distinguish what is theoretically desirable from what is pragmatically possible.

OD Consultancy may Manipulate Client
No outside intervention, process or otherwise is neutral. Effecting change is an inherently political process. As Kelman points out 'there exists no formula for so structuring an effective change situation that manip-ulation is totally absent' (quoted in McLean et al. 1982:59). In reality a change consultant is not a neu-tral facilitator, but a specialist actively influencing the ways in which problems are defined and the types of solution sought by organisational members. It should therefore be recognised that any OD programme is by def-inition a power/political event, but it should be used as the 'positive face of power'.

At the same time, OD consultancy should recognise and deal with the inherently political nature of organisa-tions and change. OD is sometimes criticised for not being politically aware enough as it often does not give sufficient emphasis to the political perspective of competing interests in organisations. OD needs to identify and expose power play rather than naively take sides, and yet consultants are very often not given the man-date and authority to do this. Team-building activities may be all very well, but if this just means that people end up cover-ing each others backs rather than addressing problems of financial mismanagement then OD consultancy may miss the real problems.

OD CONSULTANCY MAY MANIPULATE THE CLIENT...

OD may Merely Reinforce Management and Hierarchy
If it is to be successful an OD consultancy requires clear signals from the top that the programme deserves attention. The dilemma created is that this may serve the interests of the top and merely reinforce the present hierarchy. Some writers, such as McKendall (1993) see OD as a sophisticated form of manager-ial manipulation as inducing compliance and uniformity in an organisation's

'AN OD INTERVENTION MAY SIMPLY REINFORCE MASCULINE MANAGERIAL HIERARCHY'

members which thereby increases the power of management.

This occurs because OD efforts often create uncertainty, interfere with the informal organisation, reinforce the position of management and further entrench management purposes. She feels that despite the rhetoric the emphasis of OD is really on how managers can co-opt, modify and persuade other organisational members while underlying power structures remain unchanged. Others like Hatch describe a post-modern perspective on organisational change which 'can be a vehicle of domination for those who conspire to enact a world for others' ... whereby empowerment is only to do what I say (Hatch 1997:367).

Consultant Weaknesses

Dependency on the Consultant may be Created

There is a very real danger that an OD intervention will create dependence of the organisation on the consultant. An OD practitioner often has to take leadership of aspects of the organisation during an OD process so that internal leadership may be restored. The hazard is that ownership is removed and dependency created. There is a temptation for the Southern NGO to try and hand over difficult decisions to consultants. This danger should be avoided while also acknowledging the necessity for short-term dependence in capacity-building. As CDRA say, 'If we do not do that we start to lie. Power relations may be dynamic, but only if we acknowledge their real nature' (1996:7).

Limited Quality Consultants

Another major constraint of OD consultancy with NGOs is that there is a limited supply of consultants both in quality and quantity. Northern NGOs find it very hard to identify appropriate consultants with the competence, caste and confidence of the partner. Consultants are not often seen to have enough 'humility to walk in other peoples moccasins' and understand fully the NGO's real context. On the other hand, if consultants become overly involved in an NGO they will the lose the objectivity for which they were first brought in. One quality issue for consultants to grapple with is determining who is really the client – is it the donor who is paying or the NGO which is the target for the intervention? Too many consultants respond to the power of the wallet. They need to address the question whether they are there to bring an independent perspective into the intervention or whether they are just part of the delayered aid system and really only contracted out labour for the donor.

Good Consultants Overbooked
Those consultants who do have a track record and experience of OD with NGOs tend to be extremely overbooked. Not only does this mean that they become difficult to contract, but that even if they are hired they may not have the flexibility to give the follow-up which is needed.

Donor Weaknesses
OD may Reinforce Donor Power Relations
OD can also be misused by Northern NGOs as another instrument of control. There is the temptation for Northern NGOs to direct and control the process (as they are usually paying for it) and consider themselves, not the NGO partner, as the consultant's client. Because many OD contracts are still signed with the Northern NGO and the consultant there is always the danger that the ODC will respond to the donor not the client. How much more difficult to avoid if the Northern NGO staff try to implement the OD process themselves! Kisare warns that 'OD may form another basis for conditionality and unwarranted intrusion into the affairs of African NGOs' (1996:8).

OD may be Seen as Donor-Driven
Because it is often the Northern NGO which places the subject of OD onto the agenda of its partners, there is the danger that OD is seen as donor-driven, especially if it is used for the purposes of short-term or isolated improvements in an organisation (in areas which directly affect the donor). In the past, few Southern NGOs have been encouraged to look at their own organisation, rather they have been pressured to ignore it, minimise its overhead costs and merely implement projects.

OD may Receive only Lukewarm Support from Funders
While there is certainly increased interest amongst Northern NGOs in OD, many are not able to afford OD, some are not willing to support it and for oth-

ers the nature of their relationships is probably not conducive to OD. Furthermore, the situation is complicated by very different understandings of OD amongst donors which may undermine effective OD.

One of the current trends in the donor world is described as the 'contract culture', whereby Northern NGOs are increasingly 'defining development' which would be a major danger to effective OD of Southern NGOs. Inextricably linked to this phenomenon, is that at the moment the Northern NGOs' donors (the back donors) are giving at best lukewarm support for OD. Instead most are pushing for quantifiable results (such as boreholes dug) and in the Netherlands, for example, everything must be measured against sectional (economic and cultural; environment, gender, human rights) indicators causing some Dutch NGOs to restructure along these lines. This back donor pressure means that *our regional office is busier with technical accompaniment in these sectional areas. They feel that they do not have the time to know about OD. OD is a luxury'*.

When is ODC Appropriate and When is it Not?

One of the main dangers highlighted in the research is that OD may be assumed to be the best intervention in all situations, despite the fact that OD practitioners are at pains to point out that 'OD is not a panacea for all the problems of an organisation, but is one strategy for intelligently facing the requirements of a changing world'(French and Bell 1984:xiv). Nicholas in his 1982 review of 64 OD interventions concluded the same, that 'the single most important finding of their research is that no one organisational change technique or class of techniques works well in all situations' (quoted in Dunphy and Stace 1988:326).

The OD does not fit every problem. The appropriateness of OD is contingent on a number of factors:

- the nature of the need and the organisation itself;
- the context and the fit with the environment;
- the time available to make the change.

OD Depends on the Particular Need

There is a danger that concentration on 'softer' group processes may hide more nuts-and-bolts issues on the financial side or programme side just as the converse is also a danger. Computing systems may be more important than cultural change. For example, during the 1980s, Technoserve, an American PVO, established a Business Advisory Service for NGOs in Ghana and Kenya providing 'general management advice, accounting, systems design, reviewing administrative structures, recruitment, fund-raising, project plans – nuts and bolts' issues. They found that 'the demand is continuous. Interestingly, so many of the cases where BAS intervened needed not integrated and complex interventions, but rather a mere one or two day "surgical" type intervention in order to make a large difference, sometimes even a critical one' (Dichter 1986:4). (Though interestingly it appears the demand is no longer continuous as the author could find no trace of BAS in Kenya today.) It is clear though that straightforward management skills and systems are a critical need of NGOs. As was stated during a recent OD event, 'often it is not a case of transforming what is there, but informing what should be there' (CDRA 1995).

To some degree it can be argued that because OD assumes that senior managers have the capacity to anticipate environmental forces and future changes; that organisations are run by intelligent pro-active managers; that large-scale organisational changes can happen incrementally, then perhaps where this is not the case OD consultancy is not a particularly appropriate intervention.

Another inappropriate use of OD consultancy is as a life support system. Organisations do not have a right to exist. Death is very much part of the development process and yet 'we seldom have the courage to turn off the life support system of donor funding if dysfunctional, especially if the very purpose of you as an OD consultant is to help the organisation' (CDRA 1996:12).

Dunphy and Stace in their seminal article, entitled 'Transformational and Coercive Strategies for Planned Organisational Change: Beyond the OD Model' argue that the appropriateness of OD depends on the extent of the lack of 'fit' between the organisation and its environment and the time available to make the change. They assert that for OD-type incremental change you need relative environmental stability and sufficient time for change, but that 'radical times may need radical remedies' (1988:324). They argue that participation 'often does not lead to the best decisions' and that the OD emphasis on shared values might impede the emergence of champions of new ideas which might challenge the dominant organisational paradigm.

To illustrate when OD is and is not appropriate they construct a grid:

	Incremental change strategy	Transformative change strategy
Collaborative Mode	1. Participative evolution	2. Charismatic transformation
Coercive Mode	3. Forced evolution	4. Dictatorial Transformation

1. Participative evolution:
When the organisation is in fit with its environment but needs minor adjustment or when an organisation is out of fit but time is available and key stakeholders favour change. This is seen very much as OD.

2. Charismatic transformation
This is increasingly adopted by OD, where the organisation is out of fit with the environment; where there is little time for extensive participation but there is support for radical change within the organisation.

3. Forced evolution
In this instance the organisation may be in or out of fit with its environment, but what is important is that key interest groups oppose change. In such cases, large consulting firms are often brought in to install control systems.

4. Dictatorial transformation
The organisation is out of fit with the environment, there is no time or much support for change, and yet radical change is needed. Such scenarios often bring in corporate strategy consultants to impose their change package.

Certainly at times a collaborative approach is not always the most appropriate response, though it does fit much better with the NGO culture and approach to development in the community. How much NGOs should be looking to more 'coercive' methods depends to some degree on how much time is available for change. Although these times are often described as turbulent, so far NGOs generally have been buffered by grant funding patterns from having to respond extremely fast to being out of fit with their environment. This may change in the future.

Part Four

Implications for the Policy and Practice of Northern NGOs

Chapter 7

Effective Northern NGO Support for OD

INTRODUCTION

Many Northern NGOs have prioritised OD consultancy as a key element of their capacity-building with Southern partners, but with limited understanding of what it is, let alone what should be their role in the process and how they can support ODC most effectively. This chapter applies the lessons learnt from the case experience of OD consultancy to respond to some common Northern NGO questions:

- *Can Northern NGO staff implement ODC with partners?*
- *Is it ever appropriate for Northern NGOs to be direct providers of capacity-building services?*
- *What support do NNGOs have to provide to facilitate the OD approach?*
- *How can the supply of OD providers be developed?*
- *What are the principles of good practice for Northern NGOs to support OD effectively?*

NORTHERN NGOs' ROLE IN OD CONSULTANCY

Can Northern NGOs do More than just Funding?
One of the current questions facing many Northern NGOs is, 'do we have a role other than merely funding partners'. In a much more resource scare environment Northern NGOs are being pressured from all sides, official donors; trustees; partners; to clearly articulate what extra 'value' they add to the development process. Many Northern NGOs are rushing to claim that the value they add is 'capacity-building' of partners.

The reasons for this are many and include the following:

- many NGOs feel that they have been doing capacity-building for many

164

years, though not giving it this name;
- the need for capacity-building is undoubtedly there;
- some Northern NGOs believe that their traditional donor role is under threat from official donors who are increasingly bypassing Northern NGO intermediaries and funding Southern NGOs directly;
- playing a capacity-building role appeals to the Northern NGO value base, much more than the banking role of donors – 'the ultimate fear is to be seen as the bankers of the development sector' (Taylor 1996 :1); they did not join the development world to be bankers but to be barefoot advisers in the South;
- Northern NGOs with field offices tend to be more hands-on in wanting to be directly involved in capacity-building themselves. As Northern NGOs decentralise, there is a temptation to justify their existence and overhead costs by doing more capacity-building, especially as the needs are clearer from close up.

This research project has focused exclusively on one particular approach to capacity-building: namely OD consultancy. Many Northern NGOs are asking how can we ourselves get involved in supporting or implementing OD consultancy with partners.

Can Northern NGO Staff Implement ODC with Partners?
One example of a Northern NGO providing OD consultancy services in a thought-out manner is ActionAid in Kenya who have recently set up a programme with support from DFID to provide OD consultancy support to Kenyan NGOs.

ActionAid Kenya NGO Support Programme

Aim:
'The NSP seeks to enhance the organisational capability of Kenyan organisations, especially NGOs, to be more effective actors in civil society. This is done by working in a collaborative way to improve management and organisational skills. Through the programme, ActionAid is able to develop partnerships with selected organisations to create opportunities for mutual learning and sharing of ideas and experiences.'

Approach:
'The programme seeks to adopt an Organisational Development approach in

---

working with selected organisations, by enhancing their ability to do a critical self-analysis and supporting them to strengthen their identified weak areas. The support areas include management, technical skills and to a lesser degree funding. The programme does not focus on project funding, though it is not ruled out, in as far as it is linked to addressing the essential capacities of the organisation.'

Issues Addressed:
Some of the areas often addressed are:

a) Role Clarity: assisting an NGO to think through and clarify its vision, mission and goals. This also involves exploring appropriate strategies that lead to achieving the vision. The NSP will also assist to strengthen the Board or Executive Committee to ensure that the institution goes beyond its founders.

b) Project Management: assisting the organisation to develop proper structures and systems for management (in finance, administration, programme and personnel) with sensitivity to its needs and stage in development.

c) Resource Mobilisation: assisting the organisation to develop skills to attract resources both locally and externally.

d) Staff development: assisting the organisation to adopt long-term strategic planning for staff development needs. The NSP also assists the organisation's staff to acquire the technical and operational skills identified as necessary for the growth of the organisation.

Other organisations such as Technoserve from the USA have also got directly involved in providing organisational support to their partners. In their own paper describing their business/NGO advisory programme they state that 'to take an arm's length stance (with partners) was something we were increasingly opposed to' ... describing it as a 'common ineffective way of standing aside with both hands in your pockets' (Dichter 1986). Technoserve too have a very hands-on approach in this programme stating that:

the reality of working with structures that are missing so many essential parts ... these nuts and bolts have to come from somewhere. In this way we found ourselves filling in gaps with whatever is needed, whether it fits the mandate or not, whether it appears likely to create dependence or not. The daily dilemma is that the needs are so great that one does not stop to think about this issue, nor perhaps would it be appropriate to do so. (ibid.:19)

Most Northern NGOs involved in such activities would not be so frank and some would see the dangers of ignoring the inherent power relations in any donor–recipient relationship more clearly. Some of the European NGOs interviewed in the research recognised that they should stay in the background: *'only if we support their processes can it be effective'*, but acknowledged that there are powerful personal and institutional pressures to be in the foreground and try to implement the OD consultancy themselves. *'The temptation to dictate is there and we need clear boundaries to avoid that'*. Yet one of the most respected NGOs readily admitted that *'this is the biggest bad practice we have'*. The problem was seen that *'as soon as you take responsibility away for decisions you cannot hold the organisation responsible for the outcome'*. A donor intervention can discover problems and make money available, but the ownership of the problem may well lie with the donor and only superficial organisational change occurs as a result.

Just as most Northern NGOs would be very unhappy if their main donors, such as EU, NORAD, DANIDA, DGIS, USAID or DFID, decided to take the Northern NGO through an OD process themselves, so the African respondents in the research (both consultants and NGOs) were extremely clear that they felt that it was not appropriate for Northern NGOs to try to implement OD with partners. Some of the South African respondents had difficulty grasping that this might even be considered let alone practised, and commented that it was an *'outrageous step beyond critical boundaries, you cannot wear two hats as it causes role confusion. Stay away and do what you do best'*. Others asserted that *'there is an inherent dissonance of roles to be a donor and a developer which limits your capacity to be really good at either. I feel that quite strongly.'*

African NGOs pointed out that if Northern donors are providing the OD themselves there is the danger that they will manipulate the process as Northern NGOs have their own policies and expectations and *'Northern NGO staff will always have to protect Northern NGO interests'*. The power imbalance means that *'if the donor had been doing facilitation they would have forced their requirements on us'*.

Too much power can also reduce the possibility of change. As a Kenyan consultant pointed out *'for people to be able to change you have to be hard sometimes. If that is done from a position of too much power it can be very damaging'*. It may also be the case that the Northern NGO donor is also part of the problem. If an open systems approach to OD is taken then the role of the donor must also be critically examined with issues not just compartmentalised in the

South. If the whole system is being looked at, including donor role, a more independent perspective is required.

African NGOs also questioned the competence of most Northern NGOs in playing this role as the *'donor usually does not know the people and the context very well'* let alone have the OD consultancy knowledge, skills and experience. In addition, African respondents were clear that the quality of information they would reveal to a donor involved in OD would be limited stating honestly that *'I want to show them the good side – they have the power element'* and *'we would not have been so open with a donor'*. *'You cannot discuss your shortfalls with a donor. You have to hide some things. Your fears may have no grounds, but human beings do not want to expose themselves'*.

The inherent contradictions, limitations and dangers of donors attempting to provide OD consultancy services themselves are, however, best expressed by a Northern NGO – Novib – one of the most experienced Northern NGOs in capacity-building of partners.

Limitations on the Role of Novib Staff in Capacity-Building

Although the nature of Novib's relationship with its partners is often more than just financial, we would be deluding ourselves if we were to deny that funding is Novib's core business. This financial basis of Novib's relationship with partners has a distorting effect on 'partnership': the balance of power is heavily in favour of the funding agency – Novib. Logically, giver and receiver are interdependent. But it is a 'giver's market'; the dependence of a Southern organisation is much greater on Novib for funding is much greater than Novib's dependence on each one of them. This dependence is accentuated by the old adage that 'one does not bite the hand that feeds'. While there may be dialogue, one does not openly contradict or fundamentally challenge the funding agency's values and demands. In the worst cases, a partner organisation may accept Novib's suggestions without questioning. While this may be a reason for seeking to build that organisation's independent capacities, it also means **that Novib staff are the least appropriate people to do so.**

Therefore, perhaps paradoxically, while your commitment to supporting the process in the long-term partnership is vital, **your direct involvement in it is likely to be counter-productive.**

A second reason why you are not the best person to take the lead in giving direct capacity-building advice at the deeper levels concerns professional ethics. You have a particular interest in the outcome: you are one of

---

the stakeholders in the partner's programmes. You want the partner organisation to develop in a way that increases the extent to which it shares Novib's values, policies and objectives. Organisational change requires a relationship of trust and confidentiality between client and adviser, which increases in direct proportion to the extent of change in behaviour and attitudes aimed for. But as a member of Novib staff, you also have a contractual obligation to serve Novib's interests. What do you do if, in the course of advising the partner, you discover information that gives rise to serious concern about a programme that you know Novib is on the point of approving? Even if a direct conflict of interests does not arise, a partner organisation can never have true confidence in your independence from Novib's interests.

In practice when a funding agency intervenes in a partner's internal affairs (even unintentionally), the partner will tend to succumb to the paternalism and dependency, or to resist it in the 1001 ways any organisation can find to protect itself from outside. Moreover, any changes made within the partner organisation are more likely to be due to acquiescence; not internalised and therefore not optimally effective or sustainable

Novib staff are also constrained by:

– lack of time, procedural pressures and limited field visits;

– location (capacity-building cannot be done directly from a distance and very occasional visits);

– expertise (few Novib staff have adequate expertise).

Source: Burrows 1994: 9–10.

The question of 'whose purpose is OD serving – the NNGO or the SNGO?' must be rigorously asked. To some degree they will always be interlinked, but it needs to be recognised and honestly accepted that there may be different agendas.

Yet even if Northern NGOs chose not to provide the OD consultancy themselves, there are dangers in directly sub-contracting it as one of the key success factors in an OD intervention was seen to be that it was not funder-driven. Acquiescence is not the same as ownership and yet many Northern NGOs seem to be trying to 'coerce' their partners into any number of capacity-building interventions.

Is it ever Appropriate for Northern NGOs to be Direct Providers of Capacity-Building Services?

The principle emerging from the previous section is that it is not generally appropriate for Northern NGO staff to provide OD consultancy themselves. It is certainly possible for them to provide such services, but it is unlikely that they do so very effectively due to their conflicting donor role. It is important, however, to learn whether there are exceptions to this general principle and whether the same principle holds true for other methods of NGO capacity-building. Some of the main factors which might influence this decision are:

- the scale of the funding role;
- the availability of other providers;
- the nature of the need and the depth of intervention;
- the nature of the Northern NGO's staff.

The Scale of the Donor Role of the Northern NGO

The prime issue is not whether the provider of OD services is an international NGO, but whether they play a funding role with the organisation. Certainly if the Northern NGO is a major donor to a particular partner it does give them more leverage for influencing change, but the power dynamic undermines the effectiveness of them being effective providers of OD services for all the reasons outlined in the previous section.

ActionAid in Kenya, for example, does provide both OD services and funding to NGOs, but tries to minimise the funding element by limiting the scale (seed money for six months to one year); by not making funding decisions until after the end of the OD intervention; and by trying to link NGOs with other donors rather than ActionAid. Despite these conscious attempts to play down their funding role in favour of an OD role, they have discovered that *'the biggest challenge to overcome is the expectation of funding'*. The first year's review of the programme found that the NGOs had 'excessive funding expectations' and concluded that 'the NGOs while appreciating NSP's capacity-building support, regard financial support as the main benefit from the relationship' (Adept Systems 1996:13. It pointed out the inherent tension between the roles and asked the question, 'Can capacity-building activities work well when they are accompanied by funding arrangements?'.

'Volunteer' – Sending Agencies such as MS, VSO, ICD, UNAIS and IRC do not play this donor role most of the time (if at all) and therefore may be in a better position to directly provide OD support to partners. During the last few years there has been considerable increase and activity by such agencies in OD, but they too must grapple with some very real constraints in playing this OD consultancy role effectively:

- the 'volunteers' are not usually selected by the client on the basis of an established relationship and trust, but are usually not even met or interviewed by the client prior to arrival;
- issues of ownership and the entry point need to be thought through;
- 'volunteers' are usually not from that culture, and do not immediately have the language skills or understand the complex cross-cultural issues which are needed to deal with many of the 'informal' organisational issues;
- as 'volunteers' tend to be part of the organisation, they understand the context better and so become part of that context (and possibly the problem), which would reduce their effectiveness as external consultants;
- being a full-time adviser may over-balance an organisation, particularly if it is a small, young NGO. This may be rectified if 'volunteers' were placed with OD providers (should they be wanted) or work with a number of different NGOs;
- the 'volunteer' contracts tend to be for two years, irrespective of whether the OD needs are for a two-week or three-month intervention;
- even if they do not play a direct funding role, 'volunteers' are often seen by the client as indirectly providing access to money;
- the knowledge and understanding of the OD discipline and processes by many of these agencies is fairly limited. One British NGO recently advertised for an OD specialist, but whose job description was in fact primarily concerned with writing proposals and reports to donors. Worthwhile in itself, but not really OD;
- the delegates or technical assistants themselves rarely come with hands-on experience of providing OD consultancy services to NGOs, but tend at best to have general management or administrative experience.

The Availability of Other Providers

One of the main justifications for Northern NGOs to become directly involved in providing OD or capacity-building services is that good quality local providers do not exist. Certainly in many countries, particularly where the NGO sector is young and there is limited NGO experience full-stop, there is a dearth of such providers. Those who are experienced and credible are usually booked for months in advance or are attracted by the higher fees of official agency consultancy. In other countries, such as South Africa, where a relatively good supply of consultants exist there is much less justification for Northern NGO direct involvement. Some international NGOs, like Novib or INTRAC, have as a specific principle that any capacity-building activities they are involved in the South must seek to develop local capacity to provide such services. It is thought that for the institutional development of the local NGO sectors, these providers must be local, not always dependent on external international inputs.

The Nature of the Need and the Depth of Intervention

While it is clear that the principle exists that donor NGOs are not in a good position to provide OD consultancy services to partners, it is also clear that this does not mean that they have no role in supporting the provision of such services by others (in fact the reverse as we shall see in the next section) or that they have no role in providing capacity-building services themselves. To some extent it depends on the nature of the need and the depth of the intervention.

There is much less of a conflict of roles if Northern donors intervene at the more 'outer' levels of the onion skin of capacities.

For example, they are in a very good position to help build the financial and physical capacity of their partners. As well as their funding role, they may be in a good position to advise or train their partners on alternative income-generating and self-financing strategies. Certainly Northern NGOs may also be in a good position to facilitate the sharing of information and learning between Southern partners through arranging workshops and other networking gatherings.

In addition, Northern NGO donors may also be able to intervene at the levels of developing staff skills and systems, particularly in the areas which directly affect the Northern donor such as proposal writing, logical framework planning, financial management, monitoring and evaluation and reporting. Not only do Northern NGOs sometimes have well-developed competencies in these areas, these issues do not directly affect the identity of the partner. This does not mean that Northern NGOs are always able to intervene in these areas effectively, or that there are not considerable sensitivities, particularly in advising on financial and evaluation systems (which may be tailored more to the Northern NGO need or back donor's need – USAID systems for example – rather than the partner's real need), but certainly greater potential exists for Northern NGOs at

172

this level than at core capacity levels. The closer to the core the less appropriate Northern NGO direct involvement becomes. Again, would Northern NGOs really want their donors like the EU, DFID, DGIS, NORAD, DANIDA, USAID to be the one facilitating their strategic planning workshop?

Power relations also matter less where the local NGO is relatively strong in terms of its identity as well as its financial base. The poorer and the less established an organisation, the more there is a need for a neutral outsider and not a donor who might be tempted to mould the NGO into its own image.

The Nature of the Northern NGO's Staff

To some degree too, the exact role of the Northern NGO in capacity-building may depend more on the nature of the staff who are in direct contact with the NGO than on any organisational characteristic. For example, in Malawi, the director of the local NGO umbrella body frequently goes to the Oxfam programme officer for advice, not because of any inherent competence of Oxfam or because he is a donor, but because he trusts the experience and expertise of that particular person. Should the programme officer be changed, the role of Oxfam in capacity-building may also be changed.

The important personal characteristics which may affect the capacity-building role the Northern NGO is able to play include:

- the attitude and personality of the staff;
- the nationality (or colour) of the person – a white face is often equated with money!;
- their first-hand understanding of the complex cultural context;
- whether these people have a direct input into funding decisions (the problems of being directly involved in capacity-building is certainly less sharp for staff who have no function in financial decision-making);
- the skills and expertise of that person. If Northern NGOs attempt to be involved in capacity-building of partners the very least they must ensure is that they have the experience, competence and **appreciation of potential role conflicts** to do it well.

It is a useful general rule, therefore, that Northern NGOs are not in the best position to provide OD services or even capacity-building services themselves. If, however, there are no local providers to work with in that particular field; there is a good relationship of trust between the partners; the Northern NGO staff have the necessary skills, understanding and attitudes; and especially if the intervention is not in a sensitive core area touching on the NGO's identity and direction, then there may be a positive role for Northern NGOs in implementing some capacity-building programmes.

EFFECTIVE NORTHERN NGO SUPPORT FOR ODC

How can NNGOs Support ODC Appropriately and Effectively?
If Northern NGOs are not often in the best position to actually implement OD services through staff or 'volunteers', then can they support it effectively by playing a more catalytic role? There are a number of potential options:

Support Options for Northern NGOs

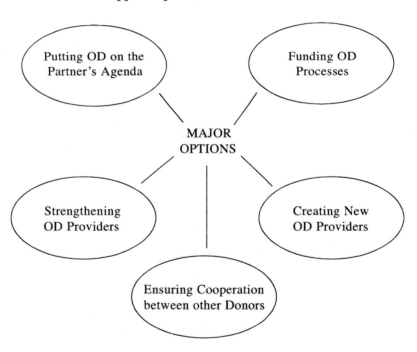

1. Putting OD on the Partner's Agenda
We learned from the case studies, particularly Sende and ABA, that donors had sometimes played a critical role in putting OD on the partner's agenda. The push for OD usually comes from dialogue with donors, rather than as a result of an organisation's own performance assessment or changes in the environment according to Fowler (1997). While there are obvious dangers in this, for ex-

ample, that OD becomes a new aid imposition, it does not mean that Northern NGOs have to be entirely reactive. Northern NGOs do have a dialogue role discussing organisational needs and sharing other OD experiences. Novib, for example, describe the most common scenario for them being *'where OD is explicitly put on the agenda by the Northern partner on the basis of evaluations'*. They also seek to stimulate the internal motivation to change through a process of internal self-audit. NCA, similarly, describe a common role for Northern NGOs to be directly involved in the organisational assessment (OA) process with the Southern partner. There is now much more emphasis on OA even in project proposals and programme evaluations. Through the routine work of Northern NGO project officers many organisational problems arise. Northern project officers need the organisational understanding to give appropriate inputs at the right moment and make the correct funding decisions. If, however, special support is needed for a more in-depth look at problems and to develop solutions then it was generally thought that this was best done by outside consultants. The role of NCA was seen as encouraging the process and identifying and making partners aware of relevant providers of OD services and facilitating contact and exchange of experience between partners with ODC on the agenda – but not doing OD themselves. Yet even in putting OD onto the agenda of clients, Northern NGOs must recognise the dangers of their powerful role – what seems to them to be an innocent piece of informal advice may be interpreted as a strong directive.

2. Funding OD Processes

This could be done by:

- introducing a specific capacity-building or OD budget;
- responding to specific one-off requests for support of an OD intervention;
- contracting providers;
- funding providers.

More than just putting OD on the agenda, Northern NGOs have a vital role in funding OD. Concern exists that there is a reticence of funders to meet the costs of periodic external inputs over a time period. It was seen in the research that many NGOs *'do not get money for that sort of thing'*. There has been an intellectual shift amongst many donor NGOs that the consultant's role has changed from technical expert to facilitator, adviser and coach and an acceptance that additional time is required which makes process consulting expensive. Yet, donors are still 'unwilling to endorse consultancy which more than minimally involves members of a host country organisation or end user groups' (Arthur and Preston 1996:30). EASUN, for example, state that they have found it very difficult, if not impossible, to persuade funders of the merits of an extended period of engagement and yet the case studies showed that enlightened donor funding for OD was one of the key factors in its success. Triple Trust lauded its donor in this role, and yet who interestingly was not even a Northern NGO but a bilateral donor – the ODA (now DFID)! If official donors are to support capacity-building of Southern NGOs more effectively than Northern NGOs, the identity and existence of such NGOs is really under threat. Such progressive behaviour on the part of bilateral donors represents a very real challenge for Northern NGOs.

Effective funding for OD processes could mean introducing specific capacity-building or OD budget lines into the partners' budget, such as occurred in the TUBA and Triple Trust cases.

It could also mean responding to specific one-off requests for support of an OD intervention such as NCA did with EWDFA.

It could also mean contracting providers, on the condition that the client NGO was at least a part of the contract, as happened with the EWDFA example. The danger of NGOs acquiescing to OD interventions rather than owning them must be avoided.

Two of the major providers of OD consultancy services in Southern and Eastern Africa, CDRA and EASUN, do receive funding from Northern donors such as Hivos, as well as charging for their services. As this funding is not total, these agencies are not removed from the positive performance pressures of the market. They do, however, allow them to make their services more accessible to NGOs without budgets to pay the full costs, to invest in non-cost recovery activities such as strengthening other providers, undertaking applied research; evaluation of impact; publications and the like.

3. Strengthening Existing Providers

The availability of proven services (of OD) is thin and unevenly spread in Africa. Where there are a number of providers, such as in South Africa, there exists the concurrent danger that the proliferation of OD advisers may be more a reflection of an opportunistic scramble for development resources, than a reflection of existing expertise and experience. As a result, there are a number of current initiatives to strengthen existing providers of OD services in which Northern NGOs are involved. Bilance, for example, are funding joint OD consultancy work between CORAT and INTRAC to strengthen church-based partners in Kenya. One of the specific objectives of this work, however, is that CORAT and INTRAC's OD work with other organisations will be improved through the cross-fertilisation of ideas and experience. Tear Fund, a UK NGO, have an annual training forum for the consultants they use in Africa, providing input and the opportunity to share experience in order to build up their knowledge and skills in organisational capacity-building. A recent Novib/Hivos workshop in Zimbabwe brought together a number of African OD consultants and gender consultants with the aim of integrating these two disciplines and thereby strengthening the existing providers. CDRA from South Africa have a relationship with EASUN which involves a number of Northern-funded initiatives to strengthen EASUN as an OD provider. EASUN staff have been on CDRA training programmes, have sent their director on an OD Fellowship programme (see next section) and are now undertaking joint training in East Africa on Facilitating OD.

4. Creating New Providers
'Throughout sub-Saharan African there are very few individuals or organisations with a demonstrated high quality expertise in OD' (Fowler and Waithaka 1995).

Northern NGOs are recognising that where existing providers do not exist there may be a role for them in helping to create local providers. Again there are many dangers of Northern NGOs creating something foreign and unsustainable, but if the local preconditions are right and there is local ownership of the vision then there are real opportunities for Northern NGO involvement. The creating of new providers is being done in Africa both on an institutional level as with EASUN; and on an individual level as with the EZE/GTZ programme and at both an individual and institutional level with the Malawi capacity-building unit:

Creating an Institution
EASUN – East African Support Unit for NGOs
EASUN was established in 1993 as a result of a Northern NGO initiative. The initial impetus for EASUN came from Hivos who were interested in a qualitative growth of its programme in Africa. They wanted to form a unit which could contribute to NGO capacity-building in the region, but one which would not be financially dependent on Hivos. There was an uncompromising commitment that EASUN should become a support unit for NGOs from an insiders' position (as a local NGO, not as an extension of a donor organisation). This would also ensure that EASUN did not just serve exclusively Hivos' partners; would gain greater acceptance and understanding from local institutions; and would contribute to the institutional development of the sector. By providing EASUN with generous start-up funding Hivos has enabled EASUN to grow organically, rather than being too tied to fund-raising proposals.

EASUN started operating in 1994 with the goal of strengthening civil society in Tanzania, Kenya and Uganda by capacity-building of NGOs and CBOs.

177

Their core purpose is to 'offer services for Organisation Development and strategic support for Institutional Development'. These services include OD consultancy; mini consultations on civil society issues and a programme for capacity-building of CBOs. It has broadened its funding base to also include donors from Germany and Norway.

Developing Individual Providers
EZE/GTZ Organisation Development Training Programme in Africa
The goal of the programme is to train professional OD consultants from the English-speaking and French-speaking countries of Africa. The training will be provided with the expectations that trained OD consultants will support organisations, especially NGOs, grass-roots organisations and church organisations in becoming self-reliant, efficient learning organisations.

The programme is structured into :

- training in four modules of four-weeks' duration (with six months between modules) focusing on
    the organisation development process
    the consultant intervention;
- participant's own consultancy projects during the training;
- regional learning groups and counselling of the ongoing consultancy projects.

Capacity-Building Unit in Malawi
In 1997 a new initiative was set up in Malawi with the involvement of INTRAC, Concern Universal, CONGOMA (the umbrella body) and funding from the British ODA/DFID. The rationale for this initiative is fairly common in newly emerging democracies. During the last five years there have been massive changes in the local NGO sector in Malawi with significant growth in numbers taking place in the wake of the Mozambican refugee crisis, multi-party elections, a relatively positive government attitude and increased international aid flows. Many local NGOs, however, are severely constrained in their impact by organisational weaknesses in the areas of identity, mission, strategy, structures, systems, leadership and management. Malawian NGOs need appropriate organisation development support if they are to contribute effectively to national development, but until now there have been no providers of such services to local NGOs.

A team of Malawians was recruited and the training srarted. As to be expected in this type of project gaining the support and ownership of all the stakeholders has provided challenges throughout the first year. The formation programme, however, has gone ahead and the team of practitioners have undertaken initial work with client NGOs (which has been received very positively). While these advisors have been initially located within Concern Universal, as the second year of the project gets underway, the process of establishing an autonomous unit is starting in earnest.

Challenges of Recruitment

Six trainee OD advisers were recruited to undergo an 18-month 'formation' process directed by INTRAC.

The main criteria developed for the recruitment of the trainee advisers included:

- NGO experience and knowledge;
- understanding of development and the role of NGOs;
- knowledge of OD and capacity-building;
- analytical skills, creativity and judgement;
- communication skills, both oral and written;
- manner, confidence, warmth, humour;
- open attitude, listening, facilitation.

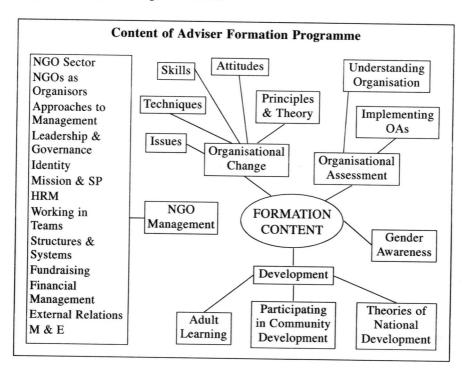

Content of Adviser Formation Programme

The formation programme for the advisers has employed a wide variety of training methodologies:

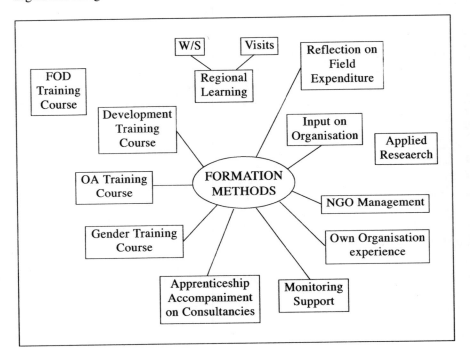

Principles of Formation Programme

The formation programme for the advisers has been based on a number of key training principles:

- practical and applied;
- mix of methods;
- periodic process – monthly;
- reflection on experience;
- participative – their knowledge counts;
- 'serious' knowledge and understanding;
- relevant to local context – building on Malawian cultural norms;
- establishing a system for ongoing learning;
- focus on development of attitude and behaviour;
- learning from regional good practice.

5. Ensuring Donor Cooperation

A final important role for Northern NGOs in supporting OD effectively is to ensure that there is cooperation amongst themselves. An OD process can very easily be undermined by another donor who does not share the same understanding of capacity-building or their role in the process. As a result NCA, for example, see an important role of theirs in an OD process to be 'parallel dialogue with other stakeholders (such as World Council of Churches) and ensuring cooperation amongst Aprodev members, particularly Nordics'.

PRINCIPLES OF GOOD DONOR PRACTICE FOR NORTHERN NGOs

What are the Principles of Good Practice for Northern NGOs to Support OD Effectively?

'Do the job well or not at all. Given the importance of the implications of engaging in OD, it is vital to give the time and attention necessary to doing things well. Doing things badly is more likely than any other intervention to kill the partner' African OD consultant.

Let the Partner Lead the Process

As has been clearly demonstrated effective OD requires the client NGO to wholly 'own' the process. In this way, it is the partner NGO that must take the lead throughout the decision-making process. While the Northern NGO may have been instrumental in putting OD on the agenda, ownership for the OD process must quickly reside in the client NGO. The Southern partner must be allowed to identify the needs; set the agenda; write the terms of reference; and have responsibility for selecting and contracting the support. As EASUN state, 'the issue may be introduced by the donor, paid for by the donor, but still the NGO has to ask us' otherwise the client may abdicate responsibility for change. While it is fine for a Northern NGO to ask questions and explore ideas, it can be a very thin line between that and organisational manipulation. Even if the NNGO does know better, advocating this line might not actually be for the best.

Part of accepting that the process belongs to another organisation is for the Northern NGO to accept the confidentiality of the process and not demand to see internal reports of the process.

Do not Push the Pace

NNGOs should not push the pace of an OD intervention, by tying it to financing schedules. OD is not a quick-fix solution. The cases clearly showed that if in-depth change is desired, it should be allowed to occur at its own pace, rather than by an artificial deadline set by another organisation in another continent. Hastening this process is likely to undermine local ownership and severely reduce the effectiveness of the intervention.

Be Committed to the Outcome
If the Northern NGO gets involved in starting the OD ball rolling, it is not reasonable to leave the process half finished and truncated. Donors must be prepared to fund long-term processes and to commit themselves to the outcomes.

Make the 'Partnership' Part of the OD Exercise
Donors have the tendency to compartmentalise OD and limit it to the Southern partner without recognising the important role that the donors themselves play in the 'open' aid delivery system.

The Aid Chain

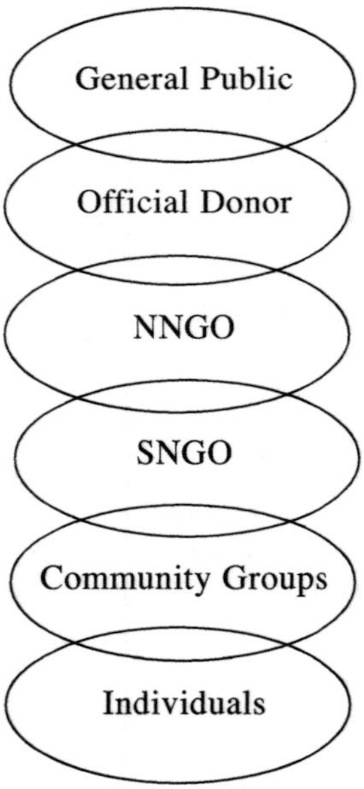

General Public

Official Donor

NNGO

SNGO

Community Groups

Individuals

For a more effective performance of the Southern NGO changes may be required in its relationship with and the behaviour of donors. Donors can ask consultants to fix a recipient's relationship with its own clients, when in fact the problem lies with the donor's relationship with the recipient. NCA, for example, when discussing how to engage in OD with partners rapidly concluded that its own capacity weaknesses had to be recognised and admitted to first, as did their historical role in shaping partners' own capacity.

The building of capacity must be marked by shifts in the partner relationship and so exclusion of the partnership itself from the OD process may be extremely narrow and limiting – though it requires a degree of self-assurance and openness from Northern NGOs which is not always evident. As one Southern NGO notes 'the resources which support the activities of development practitioners come from the powerful and are seldom if ever consciously given with the intention of setting processes in motion that will significantly redress the power differentials against the interests of the donor' (CDRA 1996/7:18).

Reduce Conflicting Approaches

Integrating an OD perspective into a Northern NGO's work also means that they need to accept that development is not linear, regimented and technocratic and reduce their growing dependence on such techniques which assume this. Donors should 'seriously rethink the way in which funds are granted and preferably eradicate the short-term package approach to funding' (CDRA 1994/5:19)

Engage Appropriately with Consultants

If one does work with consultants it is vital to find 'good' ones. Often no intervention is preferable to a bad one. The values and philosophical approaches of the consultants need to be understood as well as the key characteristics sought (see Chapter 2). Consultants should clearly appreciate the capacity-building issues of time, role and who the client is if they are to be effective.

Use it Yourself and with your Donors

If you believe in the effectiveness of OD you should be prepared to use it yourself and not just encourage others to use it. As well as being prepared to look at yourself, you should also encourage the use of OD with your back donors. There is something very frightening and inconsistent if organisations only advocate a particular approach with those over whom they have power.

Chapter 8

The Strategic Implications for Northern NGOs Supporting ODC

INTRODUCTION

If Northern NGOs do decide to support OD consultancy processes in strengthening NGO capacity then this has a number of fairly radical and strategic implications for their own organisations. Once again it is vital to apply the lessons learnt back to oneself. These implications affect all aspects of a Northern NGO from its very identity to its strategy; to its structures and systems; to its staff skills and resource base. Without taking on board these implications the effectiveness of ODC and capacity-building programmes of Northern NGOs in general will be severely undermined.

Integrate OD Understanding into Funding Role – Concentrate on Your Core Business

The increasing importance of capacity-building and OD with NGOs should not encourage Northern NGOs to abandon their traditional donor role in favour of a more fashionable capacity-building one. They are even beginning to talk with disrespect about 'providing funds' as if it were not important. Instead OD understanding and perspectives should be integrated within the funding role in order to improve it. Southern NGOs were very clear about the danger of Northern NGOs losing touch with their identity and core purpose in the changing NGO environment. Some thought that Northern NGOs were already suffering from a severe crisis of identity, not sure what their role was. Many thought that Northern NGOs should concentrate on what they do best – provide funding *'and do not tamper with what you have been set up to do – you do the finance'*. As James Taylor of CDRA states, 'the perceived threat seems to be leading away from the core purpose of the donor organisation (funding). No one seems to be asking – what is it in the way we fund that adds value to the transfer of money from the North to the South and which no government could address? Donors can best impact on the capacity of their recipient organisations, not by being all things to all recipients, but by taking seriously their core responsibili-

... ARE DONORS TRYING TO BE ALL THINGS TO ALL RECIPIENTS? ...

ty of providing funds developmentally' (1996:1,4). In this article funding is likened to the life-blood of an organisation, such is its importance and sensitivity to being just the right amount and type.

But Northern NGOs need to understand OD so that they can understand better their partners and recognise the limits of organisations and their phases of growth. Northern NGOs needed to appreciate the importance of organisational capacities such as values and let this influence their actions, *'organisations are about values and yet little questioning of the honour and will of an NGO'*.

Funding an NGO can have profound implications. The easiest way to keep an organisation incapacitated is to give it too much money. While resources are at the outside layer of the onion skin their impact is felt right at the heart. Being over-influenced by donor priorities can threaten the very identity of an NGO. In this way,

> donors should first ensure that their core activity of funding builds capacity rather than undermining it before they diversify into other activities. They need two fundamental abilities: one the knowledge and ability to understand the forces of OD, to diagnose particular needs ... and how those needs change over time; two, the ability of the donor to differentiate funding responses. (Taylor 1996:1)

As well as using OD understanding in funding decisions, it was thought that Northern NGOs needed to use this in all intervention points including proposals, reports, visits, scheduling of funding, evaluations, use of consultants. For example, just as the partner NGO should be seen as the contracting client of an OD intervention, so there should be at least three-party contracts for evaluations and NGOs should be allowed a key role in identifying appropriate evaluators. In addition, it should be recognised where current funding practice, such as project funding, undermines other OD work.

Areas for Improvement and Implications
Even if Northern NGOs do decide that it is more effective for them to play the critical funding role with regard to supporting OD consultancy, then this has a number of very far-reaching internal implications for the way in which Northern NGOs operate if they are concerned about quality.

Northern NGOs need to develop:
A Better Conceptual Understanding
'How can we teach people to fish when we have no idea of how to fish ourselves'(CDRA 1995:13)

A 1994 INTRAC research project involving over 100 NGOs (James 1994) revealed that Northern NGO staff had a very vague and confused understanding of organisational strengthening. Most people working in Northern NGOs do not have a theoretical background of management and organisational behaviour and all their understanding is based solely on work experience. Few have any prior experience of building capacity in another organisation. This lack of understanding and experience of the complex process which they are trying to foster is clearly a major problem. NCA, for example, are trying to address this issue in East Africa through the appointment of an OD adviser on the grounds that 'we need to develop the capacity within our office to have up-to-date thinking about OD, not necessarily to implement OD with partners. We need to have in-house understanding to use OD responsibly'. Another example of developing in-house understanding is the funding of this research project by NCA and DANIDA.

Northern NGOs also need to understand the role they play in the partnership and what this means for their role in organisational strengthening. There is the tendency and temptation for project officers to diversify their 'routine' funding and administration work to include the more 'interesting' activities of being organisational development consultants themselves, even though their very role as a funder undermines the effectiveness of these interventions.

Some NGOs in Europe, however, are seeking to address these deficiencies in conceptual understanding through in-house training programmes for staff. INTRAC has been contracted to provide such support for NGOs such as Oxfam, Sight Savers International, Tear Fund, Charity Projects, Hivos, Novib, Bilance, Norwegian Red Cross, Norwegian Church Aid, Danish Refugee Council, M.S., Swiss Red Cross and the Swedish Red Cross.

Develop Strategies for Organisation Development

Some NGOs are also getting to grips with developing coherent strategies for organisational strengthening of partners. Norwegian Church Aid, for example, has produced a strategy paper specifically in this area with prioritised objectives and provisional indicators of change:

Norwegian Church Aid Joint Organisational Development Program

Objectives and indicators:

vision and mission statements
- all main partners to have a vision and mission statement by the year 2000

partnership development
- to have a letter of understanding with each partner based on dialogue and statement of partnership

leadership and management skills
- 70% of partners to have made observable management and leadership advances

local resource mobilisation
- every partner will carry 15% of its total budget generated from the indigenous resource base in the year 2000

communication skills
- by the year 2000 all partners to have become involved in a process related to improved communication skills

contextual understanding of root causes
- all partners will have commenced systematic studies on issues related to understanding root causes

Source: Norwegian Church Aid, 1995, 'Regional Long Term Plan for Eastern Africa 1995–1999'

Other NGOs such as Bilance, Hivos and Novib are working more specifically on the gender component of capacity-building with strategies, targets and indicators.

As Northern NGOs become more involved in trying to support the OD of partners without doing it directly themselves, they will soon realise that a critical constraint exists in the supply of Southern providers of these services. There is a comparative dearth of individuals and institutions experienced in implementing organisational capacity-building specifically for NGOs. Northern NGOs need to consider ways in which they can develop the supply of such vital providers (such as we saw in the previous chapter).

The depth of engagement in terms of quality of information and level of trust required to implement effective organisational strengthening programmes means that most Northern NGOs will have to develop organisational strengthening strategies which focus this support on selected partners. It is impossible for one Northern NGO to support organisational strengthening with 800 'partners'.

While it may be necessary to focus on fewer partners, OD programmes should not, however, merely be seen as part of a convenient exit strategy to help rid them of unwanted partners. Some Northern NGOs are throwing training courses in local fund-raising at partners seeing this as a means of divesting themselves of any responsibility for their withdrawal.

Field-Based Organisational Structures

It is increasingly recognised, even by the staunchest critics of 'imperialistic' field offices, that some sort of field presence is vital to support and strengthen good quality development programmes. The members of the APRODEV network (like Christian Aid, Danchurchaid, and ICCO) are even now experimenting with some local offices. As has already been said, organisations are extremely complex and yet many Northern NGOs are forced to make judgements on a fairly superficial basis (for example, how friendly and impressive a particular individual is or how well-written a particular proposal). If Northern NGOs get more involved in organisational strengthening, it becomes even more obvious that the rushed field visits and bland project proposals in no way afford the depth of information and quality of relationship required. From head offices, Northern NGOs can only have a very limited understanding of the nature of the organisational strengthening needs of partners and the availability of local providers to meet those needs. No wonder CDRA conclude from their evaluations of Northern NGOs involved in capacity-building that:

> There are donors with whom it is a privilege to work. By and large these donors have a strong field presence either through the creation of regional offices, or through the strategic deployment of intelligent and responsive field staff. We have argued that a strong field presence is a pre-requisite for capacity-builders. (1995:20)

Monitoring, Evaluation and Learning Systems

As NGOs invest increasing proportions of their funding in OD there is an urgent need to get to grips with measuring the impact of these interventions. There seems very little rigour in the monitoring and evaluation of these programmes to date which is a major factor resulting in: 'in no case had (Northern Union) Chapter 12 Co-financing been used for real organisational development' (COTA 1993).

While some NGOs have now developed organisational assessment frameworks, whether any of these are used in any comprehensive assessment of impact is not clear. Systems for measuring the impact of organisational strengthening still need to be developed and employed.

As well as evaluation for accountability purposes there is a need for Northern NGOs to develop systems for learning from their capacity-building experience – to 'inventorise practice'. For example, Christian Aid has recently appointed a Capacity-Building Officer to do this and Novib plans to aggregate its learning on capacity-building in 1997/8.

This valuable learning should be shared between NGOs. For example in Kenya, an Inter-Agency Capacity-Building Group of NGOs (including NGOs such as Water Aid, ActionAid, World Neighbours, ITDG, GTZ, SNV, APSO, Ford Foundation and Aga Khan Foundation) has been formed to:

- provide an environment where people safely bounce and share ideas in capacity-building;
- provide an opportunity for learning of members;
- influence the wider understanding and practice of capacity-building;
- prevent duplication of efforts.

Each year they have a facilitated retreat in which they bring live cases of recent experience (both good and bad) in order to systematically reflect, analyse and learn from each other.

In Europe, INTRAC is also attempting to do the same through its research into this field as well as its training and workshop programme. Oxfam and the Institute of Development Studies are seeking to develop information sharing in this area on the Internet, and other NGOs such as South Research in Belgium are also conducting applied research in this field.

Flexible and Long-Term Funding Procedures

If organisational strengthening realistically does take ten years as the major official funders claim, then this has major implications for Northern NGOs in terms of both their funding cycles and their fund-raising strategies.

Furthermore, the nature of OD support means that significant sums have to be committed to non-project investment which in turn means that direct results with beneficiaries are not visible. At times the main capacity constraints on NGOs will be the unpopular areas of administrative costs and physical resources.

In addition, as the organisational strengthening needs change dramatically over time, this does not fit easily into one-off logical frameworks (like many other aspects of development work).

Most importantly, the Southern NGO needs to be in control of the process and therefore must be given the freedom to identify and prioritise how the organisational support money should be spent. Some Dutch NGOs, for example, usually allow the local partner to be in charge of all the contracting and reporting for organisation development consultancy support. This modality, however, is unfortunately still fairly rare and it is more usual for the Northern NGO to identify and pay for the training and consultancy support, although this is far from optimal.

Whether Northern NGO leadership and fund-raising departments are able to accept that funds are going to processes which are difficult to report on and to cope with the resource implications of OD remains to be seen.

Staff Skills and Knowledge

If one of the main roles of a Northern NGO is to strengthen the capacity of their partners (as many Northern NGOs including Oxfam, Hivos, Novib, Norwegian Church Aid and others have now redefined their core purpose) then the staff need to understand how organisations behave and develop. As one Northern NGO staff member admitted in the research *'we need to know more about OD if we are prescribing it'*. They need to be able to 'read' and analyse the organisations with which they work and understand at what stage of organisational development they are. Only if they know this will they be able to appreciate which organisational development intervention is most needed and which funding modality is appropriate.

This organisational understanding is vital, not just for supporting organisational strengthening, but also for all aspects of a Northern NGO's work with partners. It should have an important role in determining programme funding strategies too.

Cooperate with other Donors

Northern NGOs need to cooperate more with other donors to support OD effectively. One donor's support for an NGO can often duplicate, or even undermine that of another. *'We should present a more coherent approach rather than conflicting wisdoms'*.

Apply OD Principles to your own Organisation

Organisational strengthening is not just about strengthening the partner in the South, but rather about strengthening the whole development delivery system. At a regional workshop in East Africa, one Northern NGO was asked, *'why do you think we need OD and not you? We had to humbly accept this and realise that it was not our initiative that brought this awareness'*. This need includes the partnership relation and the Northern NGO itself. Northern NGOs tend to compartmentalise the problem and blame the lack of capacity only on the South, but in reality the way they relate to their Southern partners is often also a major part of the problem. INTRAC capacity-building consultancies with Southern NGOs have revealed that some of the key constraints lie in the Northern donors' procedures and policies. The continued prevalence of annual project-based funding is a case in point. Northern NGOs have to relinquish some of the power they wield in the partnership if organisational strengthening is to occur and forgo 'some sovereignty in return for greater impact' (Fowler 1992).

However, the need for strengthening the whole delivery system also includes the Northern NGO itself. It can be argued that the main capacity constraint in development is not in the South, but in the North[1] and if Northern NGOs were really serious about the OD of their partners they would seek to take the plank out of their own eye first.

These Northern NGO needs go well beyond those which just relate specifically to their role in supporting the organisational strengthening of their Southern partners. They are much broader than that. The Northern NGO sector is undergoing a major identity crisis at present. Their seemingly inexorable growth in funding has not only slowed, but been reversed in some cases with redundancies becoming commonplace. The role and performance of Northern NGOs is being challenged both by official (back) donors and by some Southern NGO partners. Many Southern NGOs would like Northern NGOs to concentrate on adding value in Europe through advocacy, networking and contacts, rather than always trying to do things in the South. Problems of identity and purpose currently permeate many Northern NGOs and might reach epidemic proportions over the next ten years. Many Northern NGOs are in desperate need of organisational strengthening themselves to prevent this occurring and to help them focus on a meaningful and effective development role in their changing environment.

While issues of values, mission, strategy, systems and structure are often discussed only in relation to Southern NGOs, many Northern NGOs need to deal directly with these issues themselves. Indeed INTRAC was established on the principle that Northern NGOs had to improve their own performance in order to improve development effectiveness, not simply tell their partners to improve.

Northern NGOs have not been traditionally very open to internal change. Their lack of outside evaluations and the buoyant funding situation with ever-growing budgets have made them fairly impermeable to change. The current funding crisis, the challenge to their donor role and the pressure from their own donors for greater accountability have provoked organisational crises throughout the sector which may well be the catalyst for Northern NGOs to take their own performance more seriously and deal with their own organisation development.

---

[1] See for example Smillie, I. 1995, *The Alms Bazaar* and Sogge, D., et al 1996, *Compassion and Calculation.*

Conclusions

The research on which this publication has been based provides considerable evidence that **OD consultancy can be an effective intervention in building the capacity of NGOs.** It seems to have been particularly effective (although not exclusively) in helping organisations which have got 'stuck' in a particular way of doing things and are experiencing some sort of crisis as a result. OD consultancy appeared to be potentially appropriate for all types, sizes and ages of NGOs in many different contexts. Yet it was clear that the impact of OD consultancy follows the unpopular principle of most development interventions that there is an inverse correlation between the scale of the need and the scale of the impact. As with all capacity-building programmes, the more 'needy' the organisation and the more 'needy' the context, the less the impact of the intervention.

While OD consultancy can be **an** answer to particular organisational problems at particular times, it is not **the** answer to all organisational ills. OD consultancy is clearly an expensive and long-term approach to change which, like all change processes, is complex and painful at times. If quick-fix solutions are being sought, ODC will not provide any answers. Kaplan describes organisational change processes as 'contradictory, ambiguous and obtuse. Most of all they are unpredictable and therefore while they can be influenced, they lie forever beyond our control' (Kaplan and Taylor 1996:7). The complexity of organisational change is reflected by the inherent limitations of OD consultancy which recognises that responsibility for change lies with the client and all that consultants can do is to help create conditions that make change less threatening and help people choose to change.

The case studies showed that to be effective the OD intervention, above all, had to be owned by the organisation concerned and not imposed from outside. They also revealed how dependent its success is on the individual skills, attitudes and behaviours of the consultants themselves. The characteristics required to be an effective OD consultant are very demanding – both quantity and quality of such providers need to be increased. The research also showed that for OD consultancy to be effective it had to understand and adapt to the particular cultural context of the society and the organisation.

For Northern NGOs this means that most of the critical factors determining the success of an OD consultancy are out of their hands. They need to clearly understand their role in the process (especially the very dangerous step of trying to provide ODC themselves) and appreciate the sometimes subtle difference between effective support and unconsciously undermining an OD intervention.

Effective support means to follow such principles as:

- fund ODC appropriately:
- allow the local partner to lead the process with contracting and reporting;
- allow the change process, not the Northern NGO's committee meetings, to direct the pace;
- be aware of the qualities needed by good OD consultants;
- support the development of local consultants;
- allow the OD process to encompass the relationship with the Northern NGO;
- use their understanding of how organisations develop to direct their funding policies and procedures. The theory which underpins ODC may be of even greater value than the consultancy intervention itself.

Whether Northern NGOs are prepared to do this depends ultimately on their understanding of development and their ability to put this into practice. If Northern NGOs continue to compartmentalise all problems in the South without being prepared to recognise and address their role in the process and give up some of their power in their relations with Southern NGOs, then this reveals a particular paternalistic approach to development. While this approach has been intellectually discredited, it unfortunately continues to be practised by some. Whether such an ineffective approach will be allowed to continue by other stakeholders is in doubt.

Northern NGOs are at a cross-roads. Their role and legitimacy is being questioned by official donors and Southern NGOs alike. At the moment there are significant pressures for change as well as opportunities to change. Northern NGOs must not miss these opportunities, but must unflinchingly address their own OD needs. Only if they do take their own organisation development seriously will they survive as key development players in the twenty-first century.

Bibliography

ACORD, 1992, 'ACORD's Experience of Institutional Development', ACORD/NOVIB workshop, The Hague.

Adept Systems, 1996, 'ActionAid's NGO Capacity-Building Project: Review for Year 1', Kenya, unpublished.

Adirondack, S., 1992, 'Just About Managing', London Voluntary Service Council, London

Argyris, C., and Schon, D., 1996, *Organizational Learning II,* Addison-Wesley, Reading, Mass.

Armstrong, M., 1994, *Improving Organisational Effectiveness,* Kogan Page, London.

Arthur, L., and Preston, R., 1996, 'Quality in Overseas Consultancy: Understanding the Issues', British Council.

Bebbington, A., and Mitlin, D., 1996, 'NGO Capacity-Building and Effectiveness: A Review of NGO-Related Research Projects Recently Funded by ESCOR', IIED.

Beckhard, R., and Harris, R., 1987, *Organisational Transitions: Managing Complex Change,* Addison-Wesley, Reading, Mass.

Blankenberg, F., 1993, 'The Institutional Support Model: A Reflection on the Experiment in Three Latin American Countries 1989–1992', NOVIB, unpublished.

Blunt, P., 1995, 'The Cultural Limits of Process Consulting in Development Assistance' in R. Reineke and R. Sulzer (eds.) *Management Consultancy in Developing Countries,* Berlin, Gabler.

Blunt, P., and Jones, M., 1992, *Managing Organisations in Africa,* de Gruyter Studies in Organisation, Berlin.

Blunt, P., and Jones, M., 1993, *Managing Organisations in Africa: Texts, Readings and Cases,* de Gruyter, Berlin.

Bourgeois, L.J., III and Boltvinik, M., 1981 'OD In Cross-Cultural Settings: Latin America', *California Management Review,* Spring 1981, Vol. XXIII, No. 3, pp. 75–81.

Bridges, W., 1995, *Managing Transitions: Making the Most of Change,* Nicholas Brealey, London.

Brown, L.D., 1988, 'Organizational Barriers to NGO Strategic Action', in *NGO Strategic Management in Asia,* ANGOC.

Brown, L.D., 1993, 'Social Change through Collective Reflection with Asian NGDOs', Tavistock Institute of Human Relations.

Brown, L.D., and Covey, J.G., 1987, 'Development Organisations and Organisational Development: Toward an Expanded Paradigm for OD', in *Research in Organisation Change and Development,* Vol. 1 (1987), pp. 59–87.

Brown, L.D., and Covey, J.G., 1989, 'Organization Development in Social Change Organizations: Some Implications for Practice', in W. Sykes, A. Drexler, and J. Grant (eds.), *The Emerging Practice of Organization Development,* NTL Institute for Behavioural Science, Alexandria, V.A.

Burke, W., 1987, *Organization Development,* Addison-Wesley OD Series, Reading, Mass.

Burnes, B., 1996, *Managing Change: A Strategic Approach to Organisational Dynamics,* 2nd edn., Pitman Publishing, London.

Burrows, S., 1994, 'Basic Principles and Steps in Capacity-Building of Partners', Novib Internal Document.

Bussuyt, J., 1995, 'Capacity-Development: How can Donors do it Better?', *Policy Management Brief,* ECDPM, No. 5, Sept.

Butler, R., and Wilson, D., 1990, *Managing Voluntary and Non-profit Organisations,* Routledge, London.

Buyck, B., 1991, 'The Bank's Use of Technical Assistance for ID', Working Paper WPS 578, The World Bank, Jan.

Campbell, P., 1986, 'Organisational Problems of NGOs', NGO Management Network, ICVA.

Campbell, P., 1989, 'Institutional Development: Basic Principles and Strategies', Selected Occasional Papers 1986–1990, ICVA, Geneva.

Campbell, P., 1990, 'Strengthening Organisations', NGO Management, No. 18, pp. 21–4, ICVA, Geneva.

Campbell, P., 1991, 'Managing NGOs', ICVA.

Campbell. P., 1994, *What on Earth is OD Anyway,* WUS Directory Training, London.

Carnall, C., 1982, *The Evaluation of Organisational Change,* Gower.

Carnall, C., 1991, *Managing Change,* Routeledge, London.

Carroll, T, 1992, *Intermediary NGOs: the Supporting Links in Grassroots Development,* Kumarian, Connecticut.

CDRA Annual Report: 1992/3, 'The Developing of Capacity'
1993/4 'In the Name of Development'
1994/5 'Capacity-Building: Myth or Reality'
1995/6 'Shadows'
1996/7 'Paradoxes of Power'

CDRA, 1993, Evaluation by Hivos.

CDRA, 1995, 'Proceedings of the OD Event'.

CDRA, 1996, 'Shadows: Exploring the Boundaries of Our Practice' Workshop Proceedings.

Charity Projects, 1994, 'Promotion of African Organisations: A Review'.

Chattopadhyay, S., and Pareek, U., 1984, 'Organization Development in a Voluntary Organization', *International Studies of Management and Organisation,* Vol. XIV, pp. 46–85.

Christie, P., Lessem, R., and Mbigi, L., 1993, 'African Management: Philosophies, Concepts and Applications', pp. 77–91.

Cockman, P., Evans, B., and Reynolds, P., 1992, *Client-Centred Consulting,* McGraw-Hill, Maidenhead.

Coleman, G., 1991, *Investigating Organisations: A Feminist Approach,* SAUS, Bristol.

Cooke, B., 1996a, 'Participation, Process and Management: Lessons for Development in the History of Organisation Development', HRDG Working Paper No. 7, University of Manchester, April.

Cooke B., 1996b, (draft) 'From Process Consultation to a Clinical Model of Development Practice', IDPM Manchester.

COTA, 1993, 'Evaluation of EEC–NGO Cofinancing in Relation to Institutional Support for Grassroots Organisations in Developing Countries', Brussels.

Covey, S., 1989, *The Seven Habits of Highly Effective People,* Simon and Schuster, Sydney.

Covey, J., Brown, L., and Leach, M., (undated), 'Managing Organization Change: A Module for Facilitators and Trainers', IDR, Boston.

Crainer, S., 1996, *Key Management Ideas,* Pitman, London.

Dia, M., 1992, 'Indigenous Management Practices: Lessons for Africa's Management in the 1990s', Concept Paper for World Bank.

Dichter, T., 1986, 'Business Advisory Services to Small Enterprises and Local NGOs in Africa', Technoserve.

Dichter, T., 1989, 'Development Management: Plain or Fancy? Sorting out Some Muddles', *Public Administration and Development,* Vol. 9, pp. 381–93.

Dunphy, D., and Stace, D., 1988 'Transformational and Coercive Strategies for Planned Organisational Change: Beyond the OD Model', *Organisation Studies* 9/3: 317–34.

EASUN, 1995a, 'Report of 1st OD/ID Task Force Meeting', Arusha, June.

EASUN, 1995b, 'Report of 2nd OD/ID Task Force Meeting', Arusha, Dec.

EASUN, 1995/6, 'Annual Report', Arusha.

EASUN, 1996a, 'Report of 3rd OD/ID Task Force Meeting', Arusha, June.

EASUN, 1996b, 'OD Networking Meeting for NGOs Report', Arusha, March.

EASUN, 1996c, 'Strategy and Programme Plan 1997–2000', Arusha, Dec.

Edwards, M., 1996a, 'NGO Performance – What Breeds Success', SCF UK.

Edwards, M., 1996b, 'Becoming a Learning Organisation or the Search for the Holy Grail', SCF UK for AKF Canada Round Table, May.

Edwards, M., and Hulme, D., 1992, *Making a Difference,* Earthscan, London.

Edwards, M., and Hulme, D. (eds.), 1995 *NGOs Performance and Accountability: Beyond the Magic Bullet,* Earthscan, London.

Esper, J., 1990, 'Organisational Development and Change: Core Practitioner Competencies and Future Trends', in F. Massarik, *Advances in Organization Development,* Ablex, Norwood.

Farquhar, A. et al., 1989, 'Lessons from Practice in Managing Organisational Change' in P. Evans, et al. (eds.), *Human Resource Management in International Firms,* Macmillan, London.

Fowler, A., 1991, 'Building Partnerships Between Northern and Southern Development NGOs: Issues for the Nineties', *Development in Practice,* Vol. 1, No. 1, OXFAM (UK) Oxford, pp. 5–18.

Fowler, A., 1992, *Prioritising Institutional Development: A New Role for NGO Centres for Study and Development,* The Gate Keeper Series, No. 35, IIED, London, August.

Fowler, A., 1994, 'Capacity Building and NGOs: A Case of Strengthening Ladles for the Global Soup Kitchen', *Institutional Development* Vol. 1 (1).

Fowler, A., 1997, *Striking the Balance,* Earthscan, London.

Fowler, A., and Waithaka, D., 1995 'NGO–PODS Programme Proposal'.

Fowler, A., Campbell, P., and Pratt, B., 1992, *Institutional Development and NGOs in Africa: Policy Perspectives for European Development Agencies,* NGO Management Series No. 1, INTRAC, Oxford.

French, W., and Bell, C., 1984, *Organization Development: Behavioural Science Interventions for Organizational Improvement,* Prentice Hall, New Jersey.

Greiner, L., 1972, 'Evolution and Revolution as Organisations Grow', *Harvard Business Review,* Vol. 50 (4) 1972.

Greiner, L., and Schein, V., 1988, *Power and Organization Development,* Addison-Wesley, Reading, Mass.

Handy, C., 1988a, *Understanding Voluntary Organisations,* Penguin, London.

Handy, C., 1988b, *Understanding Organisations,* Penguin, London.

Hanson, P., and Lubin, B., 1995, *Answers to Questions most Frequently Asked about Organization Development,* Sage, Thousand Oaks.

Harding, D., 1995, 'Why Care About OD', OD Debate, Vol. 2 No. 4, Olive, Aug.

Harrison, R., 1995a, *A Consultant's Journey,* McGraw-Hill, Maidenhead.

Harrison, R., 1995b, *The Collected Papers of Roger Harrison,* McGraw-Hill, Maidenhead.

Harvey, D., and Brown, D., 1996, *An Experiential Approach to Organization Development,* (5th edn.) Prentice Hall, New Jersey.

Hatch, M.J., 1997, *Organization Theory: Modern Symbolic and Post-modern Perspectives,* Oxford.

Hudock, A., 1994 'Sustaining Southern NGOs in Resource Dependent Environments', IDS, paper presented at DSA Annual Conference 1994.

Hudock, A., 1997, 'From Transition to Consolidation: Managing NGOs' Resource Dependence in New Democracies', paper presented for Johns Hopkins University Workshop, April.

Hudson, M., 1995, *Managing Without Profit,* Penguin, London.

Human, P., and Zaaiman, A., 1995, *Managing Towards Self-Reliance,* Goree, Senegal.

Huse, E., and Cummings, T., 1985, *Organization Development and Change,* West, New York.

Info-Line, 1988, 'Organisational Development: What Trainers Need to Know', American Society for Training and Development, Issue 812, Dec.

Inter-Africa Group, 1996, 'Capacity-Building for African NGOs', unpublished paper, Addis Ababa.

James, R., 1994, 'Strengthening the Capacity of Southern NGO Partners: A Survey of Current Northern NGO Approaches', INTRAC Occasional Paper No. 5. Oxford, May.

James, R., 1996a, 'Capacity-building of Malawian NGOs', ODA Report.

James, R., 1996b, 'The Organisational Strengthening Needs of European NGOs', *Journal of International Development,* Vol. 9, No. 4, June.

James, R., 1998, 'Northern NGO Experiences and Approaches to Capacity-Building', report for World Bank IAGCB, Jan.

Johnston, A., 1993, 'Capacity-Building and Institutional Development – SIDA's Perspective', IRD Currents, IDRC, Uppsala, April.

Jones, M., and Mann, P., 1983, 'Management Development: An African Perspective' in *HRD: International Perspectives on Human Resource Development,* Kumarian, pp. 108–21.

Kaijage, F., (ed) 1993, *Management Consulting in Africa: Utilising Local Expertise,* Kumarian, West Hartford.

Kanter, R., 1979, 'The Measurement of Organisational Effectiveness', PONDP Working Paper, Yale University.

Kaplan, A., 1995, 'Closing Report of TTO Organisational Intervention' August, CDRA.

Kaplan, A., 1996, *The Development Practitioners Handbook,* Pluto Press, London.

Kaplan, A., and Taylor, J., 1996, 'Shifting the Paradigms of Practice', paper presented at CDRA OD event.

Kaplan, A., et al., 1995, 'What does it Take to be an OD Practitioner?' OD Debate Vol. 2, No. 5, Olive, Durban.

Keil, M., 'Organisationsentwicklung: Konzeptpapier', EZE OD concept paper, unpublished.

Kiggundu, M., 1986, 'Limitations to the Application of Socio-technical Systems in Developing Countries', *Journal of Applied Behavioural Science* Vol. 22, No. 3, pp. 341–53, NTL Institute.

Kisare, M., 1996, 'Fear and Abuse of OD', unpublished essay, EASUN.

Kotter, J., 1995, 'Leading Change: Why Transformation Efforts Fail', HBR, March–April, pp. 59–67.

Kubr, M. (ed.), 1986, *Management Consulting: A Guide to the Profession,* ILO, Geneva.

Lievegoed, B., 1973, *The Developing Organisation,* Tavistock, London.

Lippitt, G., and Lippitt, R., 1978, *The Consultancy Process in Action,* Pfeiffer and Co., San Diego.

Lippitt, G., Langseth, P., and Mossop, J., 1985, *Implementing Organisational Change: A Practical Guide to Managing Change Efforts,* Jossey Bass, San Francisco.

Longwe, S., 1995, 'A Development Agency as a Patriarchal Cooking Pot: The Evaporation of Policies for Women's Advancement' unpublished paper presented at seminar on Women's Rights and Development, One World Action, Oxford, May.

Lynton, R., and Pareek, H. (eds.), 1992, *Facilitating Development – Readings for Trainers, Consultants and Policy Makers,* Sage, London.

Macdonald, M., Sprenger, E., and Dubel, I., 1997, 'Gender and Organisational Change: Bridging the Gap Between Policy and Practice', Royal Tropical Institute, The Netherlands.

Machiavelli, N., *The Prince,* republished 1995, Everyman, London.

Made, P., and Maramba, P., 1997, 'Draft Report on Gender and OD Workshop', unpublished, Harare.

Mamputa, G., 1997, 'Challenges Facing OD Practitioners in South Africa' OD Debate, Vol. 4, No. 5, Olive, Durban.

Manchester Open Learning, 1994, *Planning and Managing Change,* 2nd edn., Kogan Page, London.

Mandela, N., 1994, *Long Walk to Freedom,* Little, Brown and Co., London.

Margulies, N., and Raia, A., 1978, *The Conceptual Foundations of OD,* McGraw-Hill, New York.

Massarik, F., 1990, *Advances in Organization Development,* Ablex, Norwood.

Mastenbroek, 1993, *Conflict Management and Organization Development,* Wiley, Chichester.

May, N., 1994, 'Gender and OD', unpublished paper.

Mbigi, L., 1995, 'Ubuntu – The Spirit of African Transformation Management', Knowledge Resources, Ranaburg.

McKendall, M., 1993, 'The Tyranny of Change: OD Revisited', *Journal of Business Ethics,* 12: 93–104.

McLean, A., et al., 1982, *Organization Development in Transition,* Wiley, Chichester.

Meintjies, F., 1994, 'OD – Now is the Time', Olive, Work in Progress No. 16, March.

Moholo, B., 1994, 'Growing Pains', Olive, Work in Progress No. 16, March.

Moore, M., 1994, 'Institution Building as a Development Assistance Method: A Review of Literature and Ideas', unpublished report to SIDA, IDS, June.

Morgan, G, 1986, *Images of Organisation,* Sage, London.

Morgan, P., and Qualman, A., 1996, 'Institutional and Capacity Development: Results-Based Management and Organisation Performance', CIDA, Feb.

Murrell, K., 1981, 'Organisation Development in the Third World: Lessons and Reasons Why', in *Organization Development Journal,* Vol. 2, No. 4.

Murrell, K., 1994, 'Organisation Development Experiences and Lessons in the UNDP', in *Organization Development Journal,* Vol. 12, No. 2, Summer.

Newens, M., and Roche, C., 1996, 'Evaluating Social Development: Initiatives and Experience in Oxfam', paper presented at the Third International Conference on Evaluation of Social Development, Nov.

ODA, 1997, 'Malawi NGOs Capacity-Building Project Memorandum', BDDCA, Harare.

OD Debate, 1995, 'What Does it Take to be an OD Practitioner?' Vol. 2, No. 5, Olive, Oct.

Phillips, K. and Shaw, P., 1984, *A Consultancy Approach for Trainers,* Gower.

Plant, R., 1987, *Managing Change and Making It Stick,* Fontana, London.

Rao, A., and Kelleher, D., 1995, 'Engendering Open Change: The BRAC Case' Eurostep Conference, Jan.

Rondinelli D., 1989, 'International Assistance for Institutional Development: Forty Years of Experience', Research Triangle Institute.

Sachs, W. (ed.), 1996, *The Development Dictionary: A Guide to Knowledge as Power,* 5th edn., Zed, London.

Sahley, C., 1994, *Strengthening the Capacity of NGOs: Cases of SED Agencies in Africa,* INTRAC, Oxford.

Schein, E., 1985, 'Revealing a Cultural Paradigm', in R. Lynton and H. Pareek (eds.) 1992, *Facilitating Development – Readings for Trainers, Consultants and Policy Makers,* Sage, London.

Schein, E., 1987, *Process Consultation:* (Vol II) *Lessons for Managers and Consultants,* Addison Wesley OD Series, Reading, Mass

Schein, E., 1988, *Process Consultation:* (Vol I) *Its Role in Organisational Development,* Addison-Wesley OD Series, Reading, Mass

Schein, E., 1992, *Organizational Culture and Leadership,* Jossey-Bass, San Francisco.

Schwartz, D., and Lippitt, G. 1975, 'Evaluating the Consulting Process' in R. Lynton and H. Pareek (eds.) 1992, *Facilitating Development – Readings for Trainers, Consultants and Policy Makers,* Sage, London.

Scott, D., 1996, 'Managing the Process of Change', paper for CDRA event.

Senge, P., 1994, *The Fifth Discipline Fieldbook,* Nicholas Brearley, London.

Smith, B., 1997, 'Happy Endings: Exits, Withdrawals and Development Relationships', OD Debate, Vol. 4, No. 5, June.

Smillie, I, 1995, *The Alms Bazaar,* IT Publications, London.

Sogge, D., with Biekart, K. and Saxby, J. (eds.) 1996, *Compassion and Calculation,* Pluto Press, London.

Spraos, H., 1993, 'Working with Southern NGOs: Practical Skills for Institutional Strengthening', BVALG, York.

Srinivas, K., 1993, 'OD: Does it Travel Well in Developing Countries', *Human Resource Management,* pp. 18–23, July.

Srinivas, K., 1995, 'Organisation Development for National Development: A review of evidence' in *New Approaches to Employee Management,* Vol. 3 pp 197–223, JAI Press, Greenwich.

Stacey, R., 1992, *Managing Chaos: Dynamic Business Strategies in an Unpredictable World,* Kogan Page, London.

Tandon, R., 1997a, *Capacity-Building in Civil Society,* PRIA, New Delhi.

Tandon, R., 1997b, *The Meaning of Capacity-Building,* PRIA, New Delhi.

Taylor, J., 1995, 'The Soul of an Organisation', OD Debate, Vol. 2, No. 2, Olive, Durban.

Taylor, J., 1996, 'Adding Value: What Role for Northern NGOs?', ONTRAC, No. 5, INTRAC, October.

TTO Newsletter, 1995, 'Change is the Only Certainty', TTO, Dec.

Uphoff, N., 1986, *Local Institutional Development: An Analytical Sourcebook with Cases,* Kumarian Press, Connecticut.

USAID, 1989, 'Accelerating Institutional Development, PVO Institutional Development Evaluation Series, US Agency for International Development', Washington DC.

Walters, P., 1990, 'Characteristics of Successful Organisational Development: A Review of the Literature', *1990 Annual: Developing Human Resources,* Pfeiffer, University Associates.

Weisbord, M., 1987, 'Toward Third Wave Managing and Consulting' adapted from Productive Communities.

Weisbord, M., 1992, *Discovering Common Ground,* Berrett Koehler, San Francisco.

Werbner, R., and Ranger, T., 1996, *Post Colonial Identities in Africa,* Zed Press, London.

Appendix I

The INTRAC Organisation Development Research Project

Aim

This publication provides Northern NGO (NNGO) policy-makers and NGO Support Organisations with a better understanding of:

- how ODC is implemented in the South
- what ODC can achieve and cannot achieve
- what are the key factors on which its success is dependent
- how can NNGOs best support ODC in building the capacity of its partners and the NGO sector
- the internal and external implications for NNGOs in supporting it.

Some of the key questions explored include:

- *What is OD Consultancy?*
- *What can ODC achieve?*
- *What cannot be achieved by ODC?*
- *What prevents or helps it to achieve its desired impact?*
- *Where does it work well and not work well?*
- *How can NGOs use ODC or support it?*
- *How do we develop the supply of OD consultants?*
- *How do we measure the impact?*
- *How do we manage the process?*

Methodology

The methodology employed in this research were:

1. Survey of key questions of NNGOs

Over 100 Northern NGO staff members with a demonstrated interest in organisation development were identified from the INTRAC database (as past participants of INTRAC OD training courses primarily). To ensure that the research really met the needs of the Northern NGO staff, a questionnaire was sent with the aims of the research outlined and asking the recipients to articulate their key questions regarding OD which they would like the research to answer. Over 50% of the questionnaires were returned and the questions articulated form the basis for the structure of the publication.

2. Interviews with NNGOs

Semi-structured interviews were carried out with 10 European NGOs (from five separate countries) between June 1996 and November 1996 to find out more about their understanding, experience and concerns regarding OD and NGOs. The NGOs interviewed were:

Oxfam:	Chris Roche
Christian Aid:	Sarah Hughes
Novib:	Sally Burrows
	Ricardo Wilson-Grau
	Han de Groot
	Ellen Sprenger
Bilance:	Martine Benshop-Jansen
	Peter de Keijzer
Hivos:	Stan van Wichelen
Danchurchaid:	Rikke Norhlind
Norwegian Red Cross:	Calle Almedal
	Bodil Ravn
Norwegian Church Aid:	Anders Tunold
Stromme Memorial Foundation:	Fernando Grantham
EZE:	Marion Keil

Most of these interviews were conducted face to face, although two had to be done by telephone due to logistical difficulties. This sample was not at all random, but selected on the basis of INTRAC's understanding of NGOs most interested in organisation development and NGOs. It can therefore be safely assumed that this group can be taken to represent the more experienced and advanced NGOs involved with OD. Most of these agencies have received INTRAC in-house training in OD or have sent people on INTRAC open training courses in OD. Most other NGOs in Europe (though not all) will have a much less developed understanding and experience of OD!

3. Literature review
A thorough literature review relating to the theory and practice of OD consultancy both in the private/public sector and, where possible, the NGO sector was carried out. As well as publications, INTRAC was able to access much 'grey' material in the form of NGO reports and strategy papers.

4. African case studies
In order to have a strong Southern perspective in the research, a number of African providers of OD Consultancy were approached to write descriptive case studies based on actual experiences with NGOs. These live cases provide in graphic and practical terms what ODC is in reality, what it can achieve, cannot achieve, where it works well, does not work well, how it can be measured and managed.

Eastern and Southern Africa were chosen as the geographic focus of the research because these countries have the most established providers of ODC to NGOs (other than India).

A sample of OD consultants was selected on the basis of:
• experience of ODC with NGOs
• a focus on Africa (South Africa, Tanzania, Kenya, Zimbabwe)
• a mix of Southern institutions, Southern individuals and Northern individuals

The institutions and individuals which provided case studies were:

CDRA	(Lynette Maart, James Taylor)
Olive	(Carol-Ann Foulis)
CORAT	(William Ogara)
Matrix	(Daudi Waithaka)
EASUN	(Mosi Kisare)
David Harding	
INTRAC	(Rick James and Liz Goold)

The countries covered in the cases are: South Africa, Namibia, Malawi, Kenya, Tanzania, and Eritrea.

5. Interviews with OD consultants in the South
These case studies were followed up by interviews with OD consultants in South Africa, Kenya, Tanzania and Zimbabwe in order to:
• follow up the cases studies presented and fill in missing details

- find out about their other experiences of ODC
- get a sense of the impact of their interventions (through secondary data such as reports and evaluations)
- find out what they would recommend to Northern NGOs in supporting ODC

Many of the same interview questions of the Northern NGOs were asked to compare the answers and the different perspectives

7. Visit to ODC recipient
To verify and moderate the claims for impact, the INTRAC researcher visited the recipient case-study NGOs (where possible) and interviewed the NGO director and two to three other members of staff from different parts of the organisation. 7/9 of the case studies were possible to follow up in this way. If these clients also believed that the OD consultancy had a significant impact on their NGOs ability to be an effective agent of development then it was felt that a strong claim could be made that ODC has value in certain circumstances, though independent evaluation at the level of NGO beneficiaries was not possible within the research resources.

7. Visit to NNGO field offices
Where appropriate visits and interviews were conducted with Northern NGO field offices such as in Kenya with Norwegian Church Aid, ActionAid and Water Aid.

8. Action research in Malawi
As well as conducting this more traditional form of extractive research, the INTRAC researcher has been involved for the last 10 months as a consultant in Malawi, helping to establish an NGO provider of OD services. These experiences 'at the coal face' have provided very valuable insights into the practical realities of OD. It is believed that although the researcher was not an 'objective outsider' in this case, this rich action research data provides a valuable complement to the other case studies.

9. Analysis and write up
Once all the interviews and field visits were conducted the information was analysed and written up (although the research chose to give on-going feedback throughout the project through the publication and dissemination of *ODC News* – a short newsletter).

Limitations of the Research
'The topic of organisational change is a good one for underscoring the fragility

and temporality of all thoughts about organisation and organisation theory' (Hatch 1997:375)

In order to make the research viable, it had to focus on OD consultancy as the only element of capacity-building for NGOs. The temptation is therefore to see it as the only option for capacity-building which is patently not the case. OD is only one approach to NGO capacity-building and is not appropriate in all circumstances.

Organisation Development suffers from serious definitional difficulties as we saw in Chapter 1. The case studies selected represent interventions which would be broadly described as OD by most commentators. Boundaries of OD are, however, very unclear and so any analysis of OD may be difficult to compare with others which use a different definition.

The sample of OD cases is limited both in number and geographic scope. It is dangerous to make sweeping generalisations from only nine examples, although there are common themes and learning from many of the cases. Furthermore, Eastern and Southern Africa (and each of the countries within them) represent particular contexts. We saw that the effectiveness of OD is contingent on its environment and so lessons from Eastern and Southern Africa need to be contextualiesd before being applied more globally.

It proved extremely difficult to achieve the objective evaluation of OD which many donors seek. The inherent issues in any evaluation of OD consultancy are covered in more detail in Chapter 6. Again, just as the sample of Northern NGOs is biased towards those most interested in OD, so the case-study selection is not random. The case studies were chosen by the providers themselves and perhaps represent examples of their 'best' OD practice, rather than when things went 'horribly wrong'. The evidence of these cases may lead to conclusions about the effectiveness of OD consultancy when done well, but it cannot be used as an aggregated evaluation of the effectiveness of OD consultancy with NGOs generally.

Furthermore the research methodology was primarily confined to meeting with the providers and their NGO clients. The time and resource limitations of this study, as well as problems of entry and access, made it difficult to undertake an in-depth evaluation of the impact of the ODC on the ultimate beneficiaries of the recipient NGO, although in two of the cases of membership organisations the respondents were also members and therefore beneficiaries.

In order to provide NGOs with a useful piece of applied research, the project had to impose important limits on its scope. The research chose to work from the assumption that strengthened capacity of NGOs would have a positive impact on social change and development. It did not seek to investigate the mission of each client to evaluate whether this was the case. Yet as Renshaw states, 'supporting SNGOs does not in and of itself strengthen civil society' (Hudock

1997:20). It did not explore important questions such as 'OD for what purpose?' and whether capacity-building is a means to an end or an end in itself. The scope of the research therefore chose not to address in this publication some of these very important post-modern critiques of NGOs and capacity-building.